60's AND 70's

DESIGNS AND MEMORABILIA

IDENTIFICATION AND PRICE GUIDE
1st Edition

ANNE GILBERT

Photographs by Liz Cunningham

The CONFIDENT COLLECTOR™

AVON BOOKS ◆ NEW YORK

Important Notice: All of the information, including valuations, in this book has been compiled from the most reliable sources, and every effort has been made to eliminate errors and questionable data. Nevertheless, the possibility of error always exists in a work of such scope. The publisher and the author will not be held responsible for losses which may occur in the purchase, sale, or other transaction of property because of information contained herein. Readers who feel they have discovered errors are invited to *write* the author in care of Avon Books so that the errors may be corrected in subsequent editions.

THE CONFIDENT COLLECTOR: 60s AND 70s DESIGNS AND MEMORABILIA IDENTIFICATION AND PRICE GUIDE (1st edition) is an original publication of Avon Books. This edition has never before appeared in book form.

AVON BOOKS
A division of
The Hearst Corporation
1350 Avenue of the Americas
New York, New York 10019

Copyright © 1994 by Anne Gilbert
Interior design by Suzanne H. Holt
Photographs by Liz Cunningham
Cover photo by Tom Nikosey
The Confident Collector and its logo are trademarked properties of Avon Books
Published by arrangement with the author
Library of Congress Catalog Card Number: 94-1486
ISBN: 0-380-77089-X

Library of Congress Cataloging in Publication Data:

Gilbert, Anne, 1927–
    The confident collector : 60s and 70s designs and memorabilia / Anne Gilbert.
        p.   cm.
    1. Design—History—20th century—Themes, motives—Catalogs.
2. Design—Collectors and collecting—Catalogs.   I. Title.
NK1390.G56   1994   94-1486
745.4′442—dc20   CIP

First Avon Books Trade Printing: June 1994

AVON TRADEMARK REG. U.S. PAT. OFF. AND IN OTHER COUNTRIES, MARCA REGISTRADA, HECHO EN U.S.A.

Printed in the U.S.A.

OPM 10 9 8 7 6 5 4 3 2

❋ Contents ❋

❀ Acknowledgments ❀

It took many helping hands and minds to create this book, which could not have been written without taking note of how our designs . . . from decorative arts to memorabilia . . . have been shaped by the momentous historical and sociological events of the 1960s and 1970s. Therefore, my thanks go first to those designers and artisans who were there, creating what a new generation is rediscovering and collecting. They include Michael and Frances Higgins, glass designers and craftsmen; Jack Lenor Larsen, textile designer; Ben Rose, textile and wallpaper designer; Jack Denst, textile and wallpaper designer; Vladimir Kagan, furniture and decorative arts designer; and Wendell Castle, furniture designer.

Appreciation also to Jerryll Habegger, designer and author, for his input on silver flatware designs, and to Caryl Unger, Georg Jensen specialist and dealer, for comments and photos on Georg Jensen hollowware.

To Molly Turner, Vintage Clothing Show promoter and dealer, who supplied me with photos and valuable background information from her newsletter, "Vintage Gazette."

To dealer and collector Harvey Hesse for furnishing me with wonderful memorabilia to photograph.

To dealer Yvon Belisle for introducing me to his collector clients, Dr. Al Eiber and Anthony Du Pont, who allowed me to photograph their collections.

To Ruby and Louis Arkow, who still live with the wonderful

pieces they collected in the 1960s and 1970s that are documented in this book's photographs.

To Peter Max collector Larry Clemmons for information and prices.

To poster dealers George Theofiles and John Kisch for photos and prices.

To dealers Linda Gershon, who added the West Coast data and insight, and David Pinson, who furnished prices and information from the Chicago end.

To the auction houses and dealers who provided catalogs and prices. Among them are Butterfield and Butterfield, Christie's, William Doyle Galleries, DuMouchelle Art Galleries, Freeman/Fine Arts, Leslie Hindman Auctioneers, Ripley's Antique Gallery, Skinner's Inc., Sotheby's, Don Treadway Galleries, and John Toomey Gallery.

To cooperative auction house press department aides—Magda Grigorian of Sotheby's, Anne Trodella and Cindy Tashjian of Skinner's, Pam Tapp and Cynthia Stern of Butterfield and Butterfield, and Mary Lou Strahlendorff of Christie's.

Further auction house and dealer acknowledgments are listed in the Sources section at the end of the book.

Introduction

✣ Defining Postmodern and the 1970s

As you will shortly learn, from a collector's point of view the decades of the 1960s and 1970s prove that collecting interests make strange bedfellows. On the one hand there are famed architects and industrial designers putting stylish, high-tech touches on everything from lamps and storage units to functional items like dustpans and telephones. On the other hand, there is the memorabilia with a message—sometimes mass-produced items symbolizing peace, Women's Lib, or sexual freedom. The mixture includes the hippie factor, replete with clunky shoes and love beads. At the designer level there are clothes by Yves Saint Laurent and Mary Quant, and topless bathing suits by Rudi Gernreich. The same era saw paper dresses and African dashikis. All can be lumped into the look of the 60s and 70s and called Postmodern.

The lyrics of a song of the era—"I'm off on the road to adventure leaving the straight life behind"—seem to sum up the mood of the times. Indeed, the desire to "do your own thing"—be it in the arts or simply dropping out of the defined nine-to-five established order—brought about a singular American movement of creativity. Even though dropping out is thought of primarily as something done by those under thirty, it expanded to include a vast number of Americans who decided to leave the security of corporate or assembly-line jobs and a predictable life-style. Whether they banded together in communes or simply communicated by participating in happenings, sit-ins, or the various demonstrations and crafts shows of the time, they turned in their 1950s gray flannel suits for blue jeans. For others, the change entailed adopting the new sexual freedom espoused by the Playboy philosophy. They were part of the dawning of the Age of Aquarius and the growing dissatisfaction with the Vietnam War.

It would have been impossible to write a simple guide to collectibles of these times without taking into consideration the historical context that set the stage for these designs. It has been an awesome task to condense what many consider the two most turbulent and disturbing decades in American history into a few hundred pages in addition to setting realistic prices on objects of the period. These pages show the design movement revolting against not only Modern but also against the political and sociological influences of the day, each designer using his or her own approach to designs and memorabilia. A highly diverse assemblage is at the root of why these decades are referred to by some as the era of bad taste. Nonetheless, whether or not you consider Andy Warhol's Campbell's Soup can silk screen prints art, hang the psychedelic Fillmore East poster on your wall, decorate your home with red-and-white plastic furnishings and neon lights, or collect peace symbols, Pop, Op, and Peace are terms of the times. What they conveyed in their day was revolutionary, a part of the bloodless revolution that took place in America during the bloody Vietnam War.

In America and Europe, the objects created during the 60s and 70s were a kind of protest, the postwar generation's quest for change in what they viewed as an increasingly materialistic society. Whether or not you agreed with the sit-ins, love-ins, and bra burnings, each changed the way we live in and look at our world forever. The ranks of specialty dealers are growing rapidly and prices slowly inch upward. There are many "baby-boomer" shows that even include items from the eighties. They have sprung up on both coasts and deep in the heart of Texas.

David Hanks is a curatorial consultant to museums, and he helped put together the "What Modern Was: 1935–1965" traveling exhibit sponsored by the Montreal Museum of Decorative Arts in 1991. In a 1989 *Metropolitan Home* interview he predicted that the exhibition was "going to show people what can be collected, and what people should collect now, instead of waiting ten years when prices have risen."

Apparently people paid attention. The interest in 40s and 50s designs has expanded to include items from the 60s and the 70s that are finding their way from the flea markets to important antiques shows and auctions—in addition to the aforementioned "baby-boomer" shows. I should stress that I'm referring to the quality material and designer items.

Plastic is no longer a dirty word, with connotations of kitsch. This doesn't mean, however, that anything and everything made of plastic is worth top dollar or has a glowing future.

The sixties and seventies were a period of intensive individual creativity, as people dropped out of mainstream society to pursue what had primarily been considered crafts. Wood-turning, glassblowing, and ceramics became part of a new studio arts movement. This new breed of artist created a genre of items worthy of being collected as art by individuals and museums, and it is these artisans and their work that are being introduced in this book. They are listed for this purpose, though prices for their work are scarce. Learning who they are and how to identify their art is certainly as important a part of collecting as setting values for particular pieces.

Today, many of these still living and working artists are represented in quality art galleries around the country and the world. Expositions, such as the annual "New Art Forms" held in Chicago, offer collectors an opportunity to examine artists' current works, learn their techniques, and relate them to earlier pieces. From a collector's standpoint, expositions are great opportunities to get ideas of what to look for at shops and auction and estate sales.

Vintage clothing and accessories are also included in this guide, since collecting fashion was a phenomenon that began in the 1970s and keeps on growing. Now, clothing made in the 60s and 70s, be it designer label or funky, is being worn and displayed as art not only by the baby-boomer generation but also by those who wore it as contemporary fashion.

In the performing arts, music became an important part of the political message with the protest songs of activists such as Bob Dylan and Peter, Paul and Mary. Each played a part in the growing climate of change—from clothing to how we entertained ourselves and decorated our homes. I'm not forgetting Elvis Presley; he does form a category by himself—but it's one that is documented in other books.

The slogan "Never trust anyone over thirty" signaled the trend to youth-oriented society that embraced the controversial and the new, from long hair to miniskirts and bell-bottoms. Not only were there clashes between authority and the anti-establishment youth, there were also clashes in color from art to textiles and decor. Peace messages found their way to our walls as dramatic wall coverings. Highly controversial at the time, the stars-and-stripes motif became a textile design for clothing and for a variety of plastic products from furniture to place mats.

At the high end, art textile weavings came into their own with craftspeople like Lenore Tawney and Sheila Hicks, who turned a traditional skill into wall sculpture.

Inexpensive knock-offs of these weavings became a revived art form and do-it-yourself craft known to us as macramé. It seemed that everyone was making plant holders and clothing accessories out of hemp, feathers, and whatever piqued their fancy. All of these could be considered part of the folk art of the 70s.

Scientific advances from the creation of the birth control pill in the 1960s to astronaut Neil Armstrong's walk on the moon to the development of nuclear energy as a power source, were radical and pervasive in their effect on American lives.

On the spiritual side there was a revived interest in Far Eastern religions and all things from India. Incense invaded our nostrils, sitar music our ears, and beaded curtains divided rooms filled with paisley and psychedelic motif pillows. Inexpensive silver jewelry from India was worn by both men and women. For some, like the "flower children," furnishings were cushions at floor level.

Along with LSD and the "power of the mushroom" came an interest in all things relating to Native American culture—from silver-and-turquoise jewelry to fringed suede.

Yet design also had its lighter side. An example of this is

the sculptural furniture of designer Wendell Castle, who discusses his work later in this book.

While many of the leaders of the "new wave" art and design movements were new to the scene, others, from the 50s, bridged the gap and became important contributors using the Postmodern mediums, colors, and materials. Among them were designers Alexander Girard, Jack Lenor Larsen, Ben Rose, and Jack Denst in textiles and wall coverings. Isamu Noguchi, Arne Jacobsen, Donald Knorr, Verner Panton, Jens Risom, Timo Sarpaneva, and Vladimir Kagan played the same roles in furniture and decorative arts.

In Milan, Italy, avant-garde designers such as Ettore Sottsass and Gaetano Pesce, and such groups as Superstudio, saw the Modern look of the 40s and 50s as an example of a capitalist society. Postmodernism was their reply. They explored new shapes for industrial materials—Sottsass used street signs and traffic lights, with bold colors and geometric designs, as motifs for furniture, carpets, and ceramic vases. It was a time when such important architects as Tobia Scarpa and Mario Bellini were asked by Italian manufacturers to give a designer look to utilitarian objects from teapots to lamps.

At the same time in the United States, architect Robert Venturi was using signs and symbols to spread the Pop message. The bright neon signs of Las Vegas were a source of inspiration that he used in interior design in new ways.

In France, designers like Olivier Mourgue and Pierre Paulin adapted new synthetic materials to furniture designs with a sculptural approach. Mourgue's famous Djinn chair was used in the film *2001: A Space Odyssey*. Examples of this design have come to auction lately and sold well. In clothing, André Courrèges was designing women's clothing that included space boots and form-fitting sheaths.

In the 1960s many new words became part of our vocabulary. Some were scientifically based, such as *laser* and *quasar*. The term *life-style* initially defined the new communal living practiced by freewheeling hippies and flower children. It later broadened to cover the individual ways we all chose to live. Yet this was also the time of the Civil Rights marches and Martin Luther King's 1963 Washington speech, which introduced terms such as *sit-in* and *passive resistance*—now accepted forms of civil protest.

The words *hippie* and *peaceniks* were born along with the first student antiwar march in 1965. Words were often used for their shock value, whether written as profanity on the foreheads of such antiwar protestors as Abbe Hoffman or on subway trains. In the attempts of the counterculture to upset the established order of society, the more outrageous an act the better. "Mother" and "apple pie" became the displaced symbols of a changing America.

Interwoven through all of this was a young transplanted European artist, Peter Max, whose stylized art became an important part of the American pop culture, covering everything from walls to feet. Although his work was out of vogue by the eighties, it is currently enjoying a resurgence of interest, not only in his new works, but also with collectors searching out his designs and art of the protest years.

Design influences in furnishings had shifted from the enrichment of Scandinavian woods and American use of wire, steel rods, and sculptured plastic shells to the hard edge of Italian plastic furniture that didn't pretend to be anything but what it was.

With the development of many types of plastic materials, furniture designs often took on the look of sculpture. A good example is Roberto Sebastian Matta's seating system, Malitte, which fits together like a puzzle and separates into four seats and an ottoman. It is typical of the chunky forms developed by Italian designers in the mid-sixties. Made from blocks of polyurethane foam, one of the plastic spin-offs, it became one of the "creative environment" designs.

The uncertainty of life in the nuclear cold war age and growing concerns with the environment led to other innovative furniture designs, such as the globe chair, designed from 1963

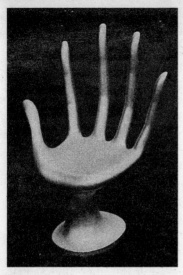

Chair, silver hand, c. 1970s. Made in the shape of the owners' hand enlarged, balsa wood and silver leaf, cement-weighted base; 43 inches high × 29 inches long × 24 inches wide; $1,200. Courtesy of Ruby S. and Louis D. Arkow Collection.

Chair, hand, c. 1960s. Surrealistic Op Art form, from molded fiberglass painted deep blue; 44 inches high × 25 inches deep × 34 inches wide; $350. Courtesy of Toomey-Treadway Galleries, Oak Park, IL.

to 1965 by Eero Aarnio for Asko Finnternational. It represented a self-contained environment using plastic materials. The Sunball, a weatherproof sphere, housed a folding seat, a drinks shelf, lighting, and a radio. It could be completely closed and locked. It was designed by Gunter Ferdinand Ris for Rosenthal Einrichtung, West Germany.

Skank World owner Linda Gershon says, "Once people tapped into inner consciousness they reflected on leaving earth—the result was furniture like the Globe chair, or the earlier Womb chair, where they could feel protected from the problems of their world."

The Forms that defined furniture of Postmodern style were hard and hard-soft. Organic Modernism and asymmetrical Expressionism were other approaches.

Sometimes the serious gave way to the amusing in designs inspired by people, vegetables, and animals. Consider the full-figure furniture of Wendell Castle. In his hands, furniture became a sculpture medium. Attenuations, also used in the fifties by some artists and designers, continued in the 1960s.

❈ MATERIALS

Plastics were prominently used materials of the 60s and 70s, as they were redefined through broad usage. New ways to form this distinctively modern material allowed for the greater variety of plastic furniture, household items, clothing, and accessories. Some dramatic examples that suggested exciting potential included Pop Art furniture and molded Lucite evening bags that took on the appearance of kitschy sculpture. Detailed information on plastics and their use in Modern design is provided in the glossary.

While acrylics were used in furniture manufacture from the 30s through the 50s, it was in the late 60s that the look changed. Forms became simplified and were often enriched through combination with other materials. Furniture designer Vladimir Kagan, for example, used sculptured acrylics and combined them with rare woods and expensive upholstery to create a look of luxury. Examples of his work are pictured in the furniture section.

Even humble household items and tableware made use of recent developments in plastics and the talents of top industrial designers to turn them into a new type of decorative art. The following comments reprinted with permission of The Crate and Barrel, describe how one designer changed the look of entertaining. By the early 70s Alan Heller had worked as a salesman representing everything from ironing board covers in Chicago to stainless steel restaurant fixtures in Japan. Fate found him in Milan with about $50 in his pocket trying to corner the Italian kitchen utensil market through a little room in a run-down hotel. As he wandered past a magazine stand outside the hotel, something caught his eye. From that time on American housewares would never be quite the same.

In the Italian home design magazines, he saw housewares unlike any he had ever seen. Since the late 1950s, Italian designers had been experimenting with everyday utensils and appliances, giving them cleaner, simpler, and more elegant lines. They were made of new plastics in intense primary colors. They were totally unlike the utilitarian, but dull, muted pastel products he had grown up with in New York.

Two years later, Heller had a little more money, his own company, and an Italian husband-and-wife design team, Lella and Massimo Vignelli.

"It was easy for us," Massimo recalls. "Alan wanted what we liked best—simple, geometric shapes. Completely functional, not decorated."

"The reaction to our first designs was less than encouraging," Heller remembers.

"The idea of using plastic dinnerware for a formal dinner, most stores told me, was insane. Plastic dinnerware was for gas station giveaways, not home entertaining."

But other stores, like The Crate and Barrel, could hardly wait to get Heller's Max dinnerware.

It was made from a durable melamine plastic. It resisted scratching and was dishwasher safe.

The Vignellis designed it to be space saving and functional. All the pieces stack into one another and take up very little room. The plates have raised rims, so food won't spill over the edge.

As Max, and then the mugs and record rack, were all successes and even went into the design collection of the Museum of Modern Art, Alan could hardly wait to get going on the next project.

"He's a hardware store freak," Lella says. "He loves all those tools, hinges, and pots and pans. That's how the new bakeware got started.

"The ovenproof glass casseroles he saw there were a challenge to him. There wasn't a single well-designed one, yet everybody needed one.

"Alan wanted the bottom to be like a soufflé, but the top cover to be usable also. Massimo and I did sketches. At first they had little handles like everybody else. Then the continuous rim idea came up. We all loved it. You could pick up the casserole from any direction that way. We made the diameter of the top cover a little bigger than the bottom so even with a hot pad you could easily lift it off to see how well the food was doing. The rim is also a beautiful frame for the food inside."

Massimo adds, "No factory had ever done anything with a continuous rim. They had to build formers to support it during the molding process. Then the production line had to be run slower. A big company would have given up on the idea. Heller didn't.

"Lella did most of the design work. I added the striations on the sides. They seem to give it a more elegant look when it gets to the table."

❋ FASHION

In the field of fashion, one of the important names of the era was that of Spanish designer Paco Rabanne. In the 1960s, as a free-lance fashion designer, he made clothing of metal, plastic, and paper. His dresses—using dime-sized plastic disks joined with metal rings—formed a space-age version of chain mail and were to be worn over body stockings as tank tops would. Later knock-offs were available in do-it-yourself kits. The original Rabanne disk dress, made in 1967, is part of the permanent collection at the Metropolitan Museum of Art.

Other designers of haute couture who did futuristic dresses and accessory designs in plastic include Christian Dior and Chloe.

Jewelry wasn't immune from the plastic touch, especially when designers such as Bill Smith and Carolyn Kriegman turned acrylic into trendy costume jewelry.

From a collector's standpoint, selectivity is all-important

when choosing plastic designs. Designer names, attributions, and the quality of the work score points.

- METALS. Stainless steel continued to grow in popularity for the design of both tableware and serving pieces. It was also used in furniture in the form of tubular steel, sheet metal, and molded and enameled steel.
- LAMINATED CARDBOARD. This modern material was used primarily by architect and designer Frank Gehry for his Easy Edges line of furniture in the 70s.
- PAPER. The 70s saw the beginning of paper sculpture and even paper clothing.
- FIBER. Fiber sculpture, clothing accessories, and decorative objects grew in popularity in the 70s. Sometimes large sculptures were used in commercial buildings as well as in private homes. The ancient art of macramé was revived to fit in with the natural look.
- WOOD. Exotic woods were used in everything from turned-wood decorative objects to furniture. Laminated wood was used for tabletops and countertops.
- GLASS. As glass took on a sculptural form it was often combined with metal, wood, stone, and even plastic.
- CERAMICS. New firing techniques were developed, and much experimenting was done with glazes. The ancient Japanese ceramic earthenware Raku was revived.

❋ WHAT IS POP ART?

Pop Art isn't a single movement but a name given to two initially independent phases in art that developed after World War

II. According to the 1970 book *Pop Art*, by Michael Compton, the "English phase can with some accuracy be described as a 'movement' because the artists knew and were encouraged by the ideas of the others: but the American phase was created by transferring the English name to a number of painters and sculptors whose work was separately conceived and realized. The social or cultural influences that played a part in the appearance of Pop are less clear-cut than they might seem."

It was certainly a new and widespread explosion of interest in the whole field of communication—what was beginning to be called the "mass media." When Pop entered the scene, this "information industry" was a fashionable subject of sociological study. Scholars and journalists like Clement Greenberg, Dwight Mac Donald, Marshall McLuhan, and Vance Packard brought it to public attention in best-selling books. By the time its concepts came to market in the form of paintings, decorative arts, and a host of other categories, the public had already been primed. Little did they know they were buying into a future collecting field.

There are many ways to describe Pop. Representative Pop paintings may show flatness, frontality, centrality, and repetition of resulting images that include everything from Coke bottles to celebrity likenesses. The total effect duplicates that of a print. Images are repeated over and over using different colors. An example is Andy Warhol's *Marilyn Monroe*, in which the star's likeness is repeated on silk screen prints with varying colors.

In New York, early Pop Art collectors sought works by Roy Lichtenstein, Claes Oldenburg, Andy Warhol, Tom Wesselmann, Jim Dine, and Robert Indiana—all considered leaders in the movement. Pop Art became popular in San Francisco and Los Angeles on the West Coast, and in Chicago in the Midwest. By 1962 the look of Pop Art began to change, having taken on a more graphic quality. It was a new look that turned objects from everyday life into an art form.

Paintings of Campbell's Soup cans, or Jasper Johns's

"painted bronze," depicting a pair of cans of Ballantine Ale, were displayed in galleries. Subject matter deemed worthy of the painter's brush included movie stars and cartoon characters as well as advertising, newspaper, and magazine illustrations. It was a time when Andy Warhol signed Campbell's Soup cans and Roy Lichtenstein, known for adapting comic strips to larger-than-life-scale paintings, was called "the worst artist in the U.S." by *Life* magazine. At the same time, these and other Pop artists were being exhibited in top New York galleries. What some still considered bad taste and vulgar was fashionable. In a short time Pop influence spread to furniture, textiles, and every area of the decorative arts, all of which saw the use of new forms and materials. Artists like Claes Oldenburg designed furniture combining such things as fake leopard skin with white vinyl trim. Whether individuals considered such design in bad taste, or the height of fashion, it represented an example of a design era with a lasting influence—Pop.

❈ PRICING

As of this writing, prices for 60s and 70s objects are neither established nor as available as those for antiques or even Modern (40s–50s) designs. Therefore, I have concentrated on providing a few selected prices, with comments about either the designers or the historical, sociological, and scientific influences that brought them about. Unlike items from earlier decades, not many 60s and 70s items make it to the big auction houses around the country. Usually examples that turn up there are the high-end pieces by important designers like Vernor Panton (furniture) or Dale Chihuly (studio glass). As more and more buyers come into the market, however, expect big changes.

I have relied on the foresight of dealers such as Linda Gershon, Yvon Belisle, and David Pinson, and the small band of serious collectors, for their input on what people are collecting and how it is priced. Other sources for information on these pieces are individuals who were the original owners or actually made examples themselves, such as Ruby and Louis Arkow, who still own and use 1970s pieces as decorative accents in their contemporary home.

Since retail prices differ depending on the geographical region where a piece is sold and the dealer's idea of what the price should be, it is important for the individual collector to do his homework and decide whether prices are in keeping with the design, condition, and scarcity.

AUCTION PRICES

Prices gathered from auction sales represent final bids, but they do not include the buyer's premium most auction houses now charge. It is usually 10 percent, plus any sales tax or other house charges. Unless otherwise noted, prices are from auction results. Photo captions, on the other hand, list individual sources.

BEST PLACES TO BUY

In one sense, the answer to that all-important question is "Wherever or whenever you can." Interesting jewelry, for instance, could cost a couple of dollars at a local flea market. Certainly garage and estate sales can yield bargains and surprises. After all, that's where the "pickers"—those who then sell to the dealers—buy. Consignment shops are excellent sources for designs from the 60s and 70s. Small antiques shows and mall shows generally have examples of small pieces from jewelry to decorative items. In particular, they are good places to look for Indian jewelry, plastic wall decorations, and Playboy Club souvenirs. In today's market, once you know what to look for, it may be wise to spend only on quality examples from one of the high-end dealers. They are turning up more and more frequently at the best antiques shows. As a buyer, you benefit from the research they have had to do to come up with reasonable prices and document the names and dates of the craftsmen and manufacturers who are worth collecting. Just remember what happened to quality Art Deco pieces, pricewise. When they ended up at major auction houses prices were often out of sight, and buyers had to watch carefully for reproductions.

GOOD BUYS AT SMALL AUCTIONS

It's to your advantage to seek out small auction houses (far from the big cities), who aren't familiar with how to price 60s and 70s items. Often you can happen upon these auctions when you're taking a weekend trip to outlying areas. Some are held on estate premises. Your research can really pay off when you spot an Italian floor lamp by a name designer and get the bid for $50. The same lamp could sell at a big city auction for $500. How did it get to this place? Well, objects have a tendency to travel. And when they go out of fashion they are either put in the trash or sent to the attic, until they end up as one of the lots at an estate auction. Another advantage to these weekend auction forays is that they are too small to attract the attention of many big city dealers. Besides, 60s and 70s objects aren't yet considered that salable. The exception is kitschy stuff. Smilies, plastic lamps, and any kind of jewelry gets snapped up and is resold, overpriced.

FAKES AND REPRODUCTIONS

Many manufacturers are reissuing old furniture designs. Popular posters from the 60s were reproduced beginning in 1967. Such reproductions include those featuring Jefferson Airplane, Big Brother and the Holding Company, and the Arnold Skolnick–designed dove-and-guitar Woodstock poster.

❄ INDUSTRIAL DESIGN AND DESIGNERS

The role of industrial designers and architects, which increased in importance at the beginning of the twentieth century, continued to influence how we dined, how we furnished our homes, what we wore, and what we lived in. In the 60s and 70s this influence came to encompass how we entertained ourselves and how we performed even the humblest task—be it shaving or making a telephone call.

Regardless of the medium, from the new plastics to stainless steel, the challenge for the industrial designer was to take advantage of advances in mass production without sacrificing the aesthetic. This is especially true in our increasingly computerized society, where everything from movie poster art to metal designs is often worked out on a computer.

A good example of the artist joining hands with technology is the work of movie poster artist John Alvin. He is one of the most successful artists in the field, as creator of the 1970s *Star Trek* and *E.T.* posters. His feeling is: "With current technology it is no longer difficult to combine imagery. I designed the *Batman* poster on my Macintosh computer with art, then documented it again on the computer."

With current collector interest in movie posters, in another decade buyers will doubtless be looking for examples from the 1970s. Will it make any difference that a computer was used in their design? Of course not. Most people won't even be aware or care—as long as the subject and the art are compelling.

It would seem that the items worth collecting from this era will be judged on the merit of their design—as is the case for earlier collectibles. Kitsch will always be kitsch whether it is mass-produced in plastic, ceramics, or any other material.

Utilitarian objects such as irons and ironing boards made in the 20s and 30s are being purchased by serious collectors at prices often in the hundreds of dollars—along with radios from 30s and typewriters from the 40s. With that in mind, it doesn't seem too farfetched to project that in the near future early computers and microwave ovens will become objects of collectors' attention. I have no doubt they already are.

In any case, the industrial designer will continue to influence what we collect, regardless of the materials involved. Thus, having a discriminating eye becomes more important than ever. In our throwaway society, many mass-produced 60s and 70s objects that we took for granted, used when they were trendy, and then tossed, are now scarce. Many represent good design using man-made materials. Stainless steel and plastic dinnerware, paper dresses, old luggage, and telephones can fall into the good design category, or they may be kitsch. This book lists examples of both and the values placed on them by those who are selling them. Some of the best industrial designers are listed, along with some of their works, even when pricing information wasn't available.

The Crate and Barrel, whose first catalog offered good industrial designed items in 1976, has allowed me to include examples from that catalog, along with their original prices. How many of them did you buy? How many do you still have? For fun, compare these early prices with any you see in dealer shops or shows.

What value should be placed on industrial designs? Probably the primary consideration should be the particular design and the designer, followed by the scarcity and condition. If the past is any indication, the prices for the best examples will only continue to go up.

❀ MARKETING NEW DESIGNS AND MATERIALS

Imagine a time, pre-1960s, when gourmet kitchenware was specially imported, hard to find, and costly. Few young couples had ever even heard of Swedish pottery named Arabia or seen quality Scandinavian glassware sold as "seconds" at drop dead prices. While expensive specialty stores like Baldwin-Kingrey had introduced the clean lines of Modern kitchenware and furniture in the 1950s, by the 1960s and 1970s there was a growing interest in affordable, unique home accessories by another generation of young adults. This was the start of the whole merchandising chain reaction that brought elegant yet functional European housewares and colorful Scandinavian fabrics from Finland's Marimekko factory to American homes in the 1960s—and at affordable prices, too.

Gordon Segal and his wife Carole brought Arzberg dinnerware, French copper, and German cutlery to the kitchens and dining rooms of America. Prior to this, these wares could only be found in expensive gourmet shops. However, when Segal was washing some of his own Arzberg (bought on a Caribbean honeymoon) the idea came to him that there were other young couples who had good taste and little money and who would welcome products that had style and were also a good value.

In 1962, Gordon and Carole Segal decided to contact the many anonymous European craftspeople whose work had attracted them on a previous trip. Because of the opening of the St. Lawrence Seaway, their products could be shipped directly to Chicago, and the Segals opened the first Crate and Barrel store in an old building in Chicago's Old Town area. Because they couldn't afford Sheetrock to cover the oil-soaked walls of the former elevator factory, they nailed up crating lumber. The crates and barrels in which the merchandise arrived became part of the decor—turned upside down to use as display cases. Thus the store's name was born! Today, with forty-five stores around the country in suburban malls and quality shopping areas, such as Chicago's North Michigan Avenue, the crates and barrels are still part of the decor, spilling over with merchandise from all over the world.

From a collector's standpoint, the teak trays, glass candle holders, and Marimekko "paintings" sold in the early days are a treasure and a bonanza—if you can find them!

You have to know that in the 60s people were totally absorbed in the new European designs. They spent the cocktail hour discussing designs and designers. What was available could be expensive. There was plainly an untapped market for affordable but unique designer kitchenwares. So in the 60s my wife, Carole, and I went to Europe to find tabletop items—glass and pottery, but not the name brands you would see at the other fancy design stores. We sought out undiscovered artists and manufacturers. Our plan was to offer American consumers these items for a modest price by eliminating the middleman. Fortunately one contact led to another. For instance, while in Copenhagen we met a leading designer of enamel and steel bowls, Torben Orskov, who introduced us to Armi Ratia, the head of Marimekko in Finland. Armi and her bright, geometric designs were a major design influence on our merchandise and business philosophy. Another wonderful discovery was some Gerard Hoffman pottery with an unbelievable red glaze—then in Holland there was Zallberg pottery to delight us.

The Hellerware plastic designed by the great Italian designer Massimo Vignelli in 1964 was brought to America by Alan Heller of Heller Designs, Inc., and became a Crate and Barrel classic. When I first met Heller he was standing behind a stack of "plastic" plates, Max 1 melamine. I understand these are now being collected, although the early ones are probably scarce since the formula was tossed out after a few years.

Once on my travels I came across a portly fellow trying to sell something called "Cuisinart," which became another Crate and Barrel standard for many years. We all know about Cuisinarts today, but at the time it sounded like a made-up word for a product no one understood!

The search for unusual and exciting product has always driven the Crate and Barrel merchandising team. And the continuing success of the Crate is based on the continuation of that search.

MILESTONES IN DESIGN

1962   Achille and Pier Giacomo Castiglioni design the Arco lamp for Flos.
Andy Warhol paints the Campbell's Soup cans.
Stanley Kubrick produces the movie *Lolita*.

1963   Roger Tallon designs Teleavia television.
Joe Colombo designs the mobile kitchen.
Civil Rights demonstrations begin; Martin Luther King arrested; President John F. Kennedy assassinated.
Vernor Paton designs aluminum chandeliers.

1964   Mary Quant introduces the miniskirt in London.
Olivier Mourgue designs the Djinn chair.

1965   Achille and Pier Giacomo design the Allunaggio stool.
Willie Landels designs the Throwaway sofa.
The TS 502 portable radio for Brionvega is designed by Richard Sapper and Mark Zanuso. They also design the Grillo folding telephone for Italtel.

1966   Experimental furniture designed by Ettore Sottsass.
The Eclisse lamp is designed by Vico Magistretti for Artemide.
Demonstrations against American bombardments in South Vietnam begin.

1967   Wernher von Braun designs the Saturn rocket for NASA.
Roger Vadim produces *Barbarella*.
Dr. Christiaan Barnard performs the first human heart transplant (South Africa).

1968   The Sacco chair is designed by Gatti, Paolini, Teodoro.
Martin Luther King and Robert Kennedy are both assassinated.

1969 Ettore Sottsass and Perry King design the Valentine portable typewriter.
Enzo Mari designs reversible vases.
Start of body art in France and Austria.
Woodstock Festival.
Apollo 11 and 12; American astronaut Neil Armstrong is the first man to walk on the moon.
The first U.S. troops withdraw from Vietnam.

1970 Asymmetric storage units are designed by Shiro Kuramata.
Telefunken produces the first videodisc.
Richard Sapper and Marco Zanuso design the Terraillon kitchen scales.
Joe Colombo designs the Birillo stool.
Joe Colombo designs an open armoire with wheels.
Carlo Scarpa designs the Doge bureau (acrylic table).
Guy de Rougemont creates sculptural lamps.

1971 The Tizio lamp is designed by Richard Sapper.
The Moloch floor lamp is designed by Gaetano Pesce.
First commercial fax machine is produced.

1974 Charles Jencks is the first to use the term "Postmodern."

1975 The Bic disposable razor becomes available.

1976 The Break armchair is designed by Mario Bellini.

1977 Studio Alchimia shows its first furniture collection.
George Lucas produces *Star Wars*.

1979 The 9090 expresso coffee machine is designed by Richard Sapper.
The Vertebra chair is designed by Emilio Ambasz.

Ceramics

❋ Art Pottery

The art pottery movement that began in the United States in Cincinnati, Ohio, in 1871 continued to expand and evolve through the Art Deco period to encompass the Modern and early Postmodern movements. It is well documented in *Art Pottery of the United States* by Paul Evans, published by Everybody's Press of Hanover, Pennsylvania. Evans describes art pottery as "not identified by particular styles or techniques, specific operation, or span of years, but rather by the philosophy or attitude of the individuals involved in its execution." Whereas industrial or production pieces required many different people for each step, the studio potters worked either by themselves or with a partner—as is the case for both Gertrud and Otto Natzler and Mary and Edwin Scheier.

Early in the 1950s many potters' work showed a strong Scandinavian influence. Abstract Expressionism and various philosophical movements—such as Zen, which was popular in the mid-1950s—influenced potters like Peter Voulkos. For other potters, such as Hawaiian-born Toshiki Takaezu, the British potter Bernard Leach was a strong influence. Leach used many Oriental approaches to glazes, forms, and designs. Like others, Takaezu later studied at the Cranbrook Academy of Art and then with Harvey Littleton at the University of Wisconsin from 1945 to 1955. His mid-twentieth-century work shows the influence of Zen and Abstract Expressionism.

Many of these artists continued to work into the 1960s and 1970s, continually exploring new techniques. Among them were Ruth Duckworth, Peter Voulkos, Paul Soldner, Toshiko Takaezu, and Laura Andreson.

❋ American Ceramics ❋

Ruth Duckworth (1919–   )
Ruth Duckworth was born in West Germany and was educated at the Liverpool School of Art in England from 1936 to 1940 and

at the Central School of Arts and Crafts in London beginning in 1956. She also studied with Hans Coper. Her work is in collections in the American Craft Museum in New York, the Institute of Chicago, the Museum of Contemporary Art in Chicago, and the National Museum of Art in Kyoto, Japan.

PRICES

Vessel, c. 1975. Glazed porcelain; signed; 9 inches high; $1,100.

JUNE KAPOS (1927–   )

June Kapos attended Indiana University at Bloomington and received her B.S. in 1951.

PRICES

Seed Vase, c. 1964. Glazed ceramic; 19 inches high; $800.

GERTRUD NATZLER (1908–1971) and
OTTO NATZLER (1908–   )

Considered the most creative of the mid-twentieth-century studio potters, the Natzlers left Vienna in 1938 for America. Prior to this, Otto studied at the National Training Center for the Textile Industry in 1927 and at Franz Iskra's workshop in Vienna in 1933. Gertrud also studied at Iskra's workshop. She and Otto worked collaboratively from 1935 to 1971. They opened a studio in California, where their small pots were influenced by the simple forms of glazed stonewares made in China during the Sung Dynasty. The hallmark of their work is the textural quality of many of their glazes. Always experimenting, they developed not only unique glazes but also one of their best known colors—bright apple-green, which has been used since 1960. Their work is in collections at the American Craft Museum and the Museum of Modern Art in New York City; the Art

Institute of Chicago; the Cranbrook Academy of Art Museum in Bloomfield Hills, Michigan; Everson Museum of Art in Syracuse, New York; Los Angeles County Museum of Art in California; and the Phoenix Art Museum in Arizona.

PRICES

Glazed Earthenware Bowl, by Gertrud and Otto Natzler, c. 1960. Hemispherical vessel raised on a low foot in green and brown crystalline glaze; signed in oxide "NATZLER"; typed label "J105"; 3½ inches high × 7⅝ inches in diameter; $1,380.

"Vert de Lune" Glazed Earthenware Bowl, by Gertrud and Otto Natzler, 1962. Square form with sides drawn in and yellow-green glaze with brown at edges; marked "NATZLER" on base; 2½ inches high × 4¾ inches in diameter; $750.

MARY SCHEIER (1910–) and EDWIN SCHEIER (1910–)
In the 1950s it was the work of the Scheiers that influenced the look of American studio pottery. Their work can be recognized by designs incised into the clay or by the glaze, which is known as sgraffito. These designs were sometimes abstract and clearly influenced by Joan Miró. Other times they used biblical themes in a primitive and linear graphic style. They worked in Oaxaca, Mexico.

PRICES

Vase, c. 1960. Midnight-blue vase with speckled interior; brown-and-white speckled exterior with abstract figural decoration in relief; 9 inches high × 7 inches in diameter; mint condition; $120.

PAUL A. SOLDNER (1921–)
Paul Soldner received his B.A. from Bluffton College in Ohio in 1946 and went on to the University of Colorado, where he

Earthenware Bowl, by Edwin and Mary Scheier, c. 1960. Mat glaze-ground decorated with sgraffito and molded fish with people with blue glaze, blue glaze interior, incised Scheier; 7¼ inches high × 7¾ inches in diameter; $1,500–2,000. Courtesy of Skinner Inc., Boston/Bolton, MA.

earned his M.A. in 1954. The Los Angeles County Art Institute presented him with his M.F.A. in 1959. Although he is considered one of the most important contributors to the 1950s ceramics revolution, his contemporary works are equally collectible. He began annual one-man exhibits starting in 1956 at the Lang Gallery at Scripps College in California. He also taught at Scripps until his recent retirement, when he moved to Aspen, Colorado. His work endlessly reinvented itself with new approaches to the medium of ceramics, and it is in collections of the American Craft Museum in New York; the Museum of Fine Arts in Boston; the National Museum of History and Technology; the Smithsonian Institution in Washington, D.C.; and the Philadelphia Museum of Art.

PRICES

Wall Plaque, 1973. Raku fired earthenware; executed when Soldner was conducting a workshop at the Good Earth Clay, Inc. in Kansas City, Missouri; 24 inches long; $2,000.

Vase, c. 1960. Raku fired earthenware; 9½ inches high; $2,000.

Toshiki Takaezu (1922–   )

This Hawaiian artist studied with Maija Grotell, Marianne Strengell, and others. His education includes instruction at the Academy of the Arts in Hawaii; the University of Hawaii; and the Cranbrook Academy of Art (1951–1953) in Bloomfield Hills, Michigan. His work is in collections at the American Craft Museum in New York, the Cleveland Museum of Art in Ohio, the Museum of Fine Arts in Boston, and the Philadelphia Museum of Art.

PRICES

Untitled, c. 1970. Glazed porcelain; signed; 5 inches high; $800.

Eva Polanyi Stricker Zeisel (1906–   )

Over her many years as a ceramics designer she has been one of the most influential contributors to the modern movement. Her early training as a traditional potter in her native Hungary was followed by her adoption of the International style when she began working in Germany in the late 1920s. She worked in various cities in the Soviet Republic until the Stalinist purges, when she returned to Hungary, only to be forced to escape from the Nazis, arriving in New York in 1938. She was eventually commissioned to design a dinner service for Castleton China, sponsored by the Museum of Modern Art. After the war, when it was finally made, Museum dinnerware was introduced to the public as "the first Modernist porcelain dinnerware in the United States." Zeisel's Town and Country dinnerware and Tomorrow's Classic dinnerware, made by Hall China, were very popular and sold well. Over the years she has designed for many china manufacturers here in the United States and abroad. They include Rosenthal (West Germany), Noritake

(Japan), and Mancioli (Italy). She also turned her talents to designing an experimental aluminum-and-steel chair and bio-morphic Plexiglas serving pieces.

Her line of informal dinnerware designed in 1963 was man-ufactured by the Hyalyn Porcelain Company of Hickory, North Carolina, in 1964. The pieces are marked on the bottom in raised lettering—"Z" with piece number and "USA." In 1963 she also designed a line of dinnerware for Noritake in Japan that was never produced. She is still working, and received the Brooklyn Museum Modernism "Design Award for Lifetime Achievement" in 1992.

❀ OTHER AMERICAN ART POTTERY DESIGNS ❀

PRICES

Glazed Pottery Plinth, by Susan and Stephen Kemenyffy, c. 1970. Two-part form with triangular base and top with organic protrusions and decorated with sgraffito and selective glazing depicting three portrayals of women; artist inscribed; 44 inches high × 16⅛ inches wide; $412.

Glazed Stoneware Vase, by Harrison McIntosh, c. 1960. Red stoneware; bulbous vessel raised on tapering cylindrical base; in mottled green glass with iron oxide rim; impressed "HM" monogram; retains original paper label; 10¾ inches high; $460.

Stoneware Pot, by Daniel Rhodes, c. 1960. Footed, irregular bulbous vessel in cream, brown, and terra-cotta tones with inte-rior glazed in chocolate brown; signed "RHODES"; 7⅛ inches high; $172.

Studio Art Pottery Vase. Cylindrical form decorated with three men depicted working out; in yellow with black outlines and blue background; 16¾ inches high × 2⅜ inches in diameter; $220.

❀ THE CALIFORNIANS ❀

When we think of Californian pottery, what comes to mind first are the mass-produced and mostly inexpensive pieces. How-

Vase, unknown maker, c. 1960s. Extremely stylized bird form with heavily textured glaze and biomorphic decoration; 24 inches high × 20 inches in diameter; $260. Courtesy of Treadway Galleries.

ever, along with growing interest in 40s and 50s designers and craftsmen, there is a new appreciation for 60s and 70s California studio potters who perfected techniques in earthenware, stoneware, and porcelain. Among the most important is Laura Andreson, whose work is achieving ever higher prices as collectors zero in.

LAURA ANDRESON (1902–)

A pioneer in California ceramics, this San Bernardino, California, native studied and taught at UCLA, experimenting with new techniques. Her pieces show the influences of her trips to Scandinavia and throughout the world. She was associated with many well-known potters, such as Gertrud and Otto Natzler and Vivika and Otto Heino. Her works have been included in many exhibitions and are represented in private and public collections.

PRICES

Bowl, 1973. Wide circular bowl on cylindrical stem and spreading foot; olive-green and crackled metallic rust-red glaze; incised "LAURA ANDRESON 73" in script; 11¼ inches in diameter; $460.

PETER VOULKOS (1924–   )

One of America's most influential studio potters from the 1950s through the 1970s, Voulkos began his education in his native Montana, at Montana State University. While majoring in painting, a required course in ceramics changed the direction of his career. In 1952 he received his master's of fine arts degree in sculpture at the California College of Arts and Crafts. His work was influenced early on by Abstract Expressionism. His ceramic sculptures, always large, were often eight feet high. He continuously experimented with new techniques, slashing surfaces, allowing slips and glazes to flow freely. Often his pieces are vertically stacked; other times he has used the plate as a basic form, enlarging it and turning it into a ceramic sculpture.

In 1960 he began bronze casting, which allowed him to create even larger pieces than he had in pottery.

In 1968 Voulkos began working once again in ceramics, concentrating on the large plate form, sometimes pierced, other times split and glued with epoxy.

PRICES

Plate, 1973. Wood-fired stoneware and porcelain; signed and dated; 18 inches in diameter; $6,500.

Arabia Oy

Founded in Finland in 1873 as a subsidiary of the Swedish Rorstrand pottery, Arabia Oy became the country's most important pottery. By 1916 Finnish geometric designs had come into their own and the firm was purchased by three Finnish businessmen. The firm again changed hands and was German-owned from 1924 to 1927, when it again passed into Finnish ownership. The company gained recognition after World War II, with the arrival of Kaj Franck as chief designer in 1945. By 1952 Modern designs were used for dinner and art wares. Some of the top artware names from that era are Kylikki Saimenhaara, known primarily for his use of glazes, and Taisto Kaasinen, known for distinctive sculptural forms.

In the 1960s and 1970s the company continued to make both artwares and production pieces that showed the Postmodern influences of bold glazes and forms.

Ettore Sottsass (1917–   )

Though he was born in Innsbruck, Austria, Sottsass became one of Italy's top designers and a leader of the 60s radical design movement. He turned his back on the functionalism of the 50s, and expressed this in his ceramics as well as in his furniture designs. This architect and designer was recognized early for his innovative industrial designs, among them Olivetti typewriters and office furniture.

The ceramic pieces he designed from 1957 to 1959 are considered an important development in his career as a sculptor and designer. Using architectural forms, he often incorporated the bold colors and horizontal stripes he had become acquainted with in the mid-50s with the American Abstract Expressionists and Color Field painters.

In the sixties some of his important designs included furniture. A few of his best known pieces are the Lucrezia bench

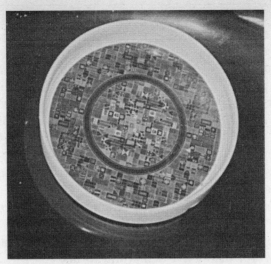

Ash Tray, designed by Baushauer for Rosenthal Studio Linie, c. 1960s.
Black and gold optic design, porcelain; 7½ inches in diameter; $40.
Courtesy of Anthony Du Pont Collection.

with tip-up seat, in walnut and white lacquer; and the Mickey Mouse table in ABS plastic and chair with stainproof upholstery from 1971.

Many of his pieces show a variety of influences from Egyptian to Neoclassical.

Fashions

If the postwar fashions of the late 40s, with the longer full skirts of Christian Dior, were right for the organic designs of that era, then the radical and often shocking looks of the 60s and 70s were similarly appropriate for their day. From the topless bathing suits and dresses of Rudi Gernreich to the minidresses and baby doll looks of André Courrèges or Mary Quant, these designs were what a new generation wanted to wear. Somehow they went with the revolutionary events, music, and even furnishings that marked the mood of the 60s and 70s.

The roots of what was soon to be known as the "fashion revolution" began in the late 1950s, when English designer Mary Quant opened Quant's Bazaar boutique. By the 60s Quant and her husband, Alexander Plunket Greene, had become partners in a business venture that spanned the world. It was based on miniskirts, boots, and "women's lib."

The founder of the Biba Postal Boutique, Barbara Hulanicki, brought the "Mod" look to the working class youth with her affordable "total look" fashions.

The "liberated" unstructured suits for women by Geoffrey Beene and the "minis" of Mary Quant were joined by the colorful clothing and accessories of another English designer, Zandra Rhodes.

When the Beatles came to America, they brought the Mod fashions with them. Men's and women's fashions centered around the stores and boutiques of Carnaby Street in London.

For the moment, at least, France had lost its dominance in the fashion world, as the sometimes outrageous designs were geared to the young and the middle class, rather than the wealthy. Of course, many of the important French designers of the 50s, such as Christian Dior, continued working into the 60s. Dior incorporated glittering plastic sequins and futuristic motifs into his mini cocktail dresses. But many of the important names in French couture had lost touch with the changing times of the 60s. The era of haute couture seemed to have ended. It was André Courrèges who is credited with bringing it back in 1964 by designing pants for every occasion and turning the mini into high fashion for the working woman.

In the 1970s Yves Saint Laurent gave new relevancy to the French fashion scene with the opening of his Rive Gauche in 1971. Earlier, in 1966, he had introduced see-through cocktail dresses and had adapted some clothing ideas from American army-navy stores.

Other influentials such as Pierre Cardin, Hubert de Givenchy, and Emmanuel Ungaro became part of the new French look.

Italy gave us the Gucci look, as well as signature scarves, shoes, and accessories.

In America during the early 60s the New York fashion industry still looked to Paris. In 1965 the winds of change swept in when Paul Young, who had been merchandising the Pop look in fashion, opened Paraphernalia between 66th and 67th streets on Madison Avenue. Among the designers whose fashions were sold there were Betsey Johnson and Deanna Littell. The newer and more unorthodox the materials, the better. Some of the plastics glowed in the dark. Others used Pop and Op Art motifs adapted from the works of Pop and Minimalist artists. One example, designed in jersey by Joel Schumacher for Paraphernalia, used Robert Indiana's L-O-V-E emblem.

One of the most popular designs in the sixties was the Stars and Stripes, used in yard goods and by designers such as Deanna Littell.

Another of Paraphernalia's designers, Elsa Stone, had a penchant for paper dresses cut like the popular A-line fabric dresses. While they weren't made to last, fortunately some did, and they sell in the high hundreds and up at vintage clothing shows.

Evening fashions became geared to the theatrical settings and flashing stroboscopic lighting of the new discotheques. Among the most eccentric of the designers was Tiger Morse, whose creations embraced psychedelic and Pop motifs on vinyl.

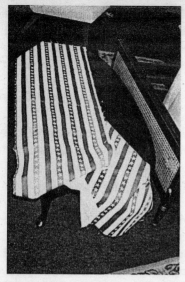

Fabric, "Stars and Stripes," c. 1960s. Red, white, and blue, cotton;
3 yards; $45. Courtesy of The Time Machine.

Paper Caftan. Spun-bonded polyester, "throw-away-wash a few times,"
blues, pinks, psychedelic, original tag: STELLA FAGIN DESIGN, REEMAY; *$250.*
Courtesy of The Time Machine.

On the West Coast, San Francisco and Haight-Ashbury brought the look of hippie fashions into vogue. One designer who symbolized the look was Linda Gravenites. In the Los Angeles area, designer Rudi Gernreich became the king of "shock" with his see-through blouses made of lacquered chiffon and his topless bathing suits. Another rebel designer was Holly Harp, who specialized in tie-dyed and hand-painted clothes.

Everywhere, blue jeans became the fashion of the day for men and women, and denim "everything" seemed just right for the counterculture look.

✽ Fancy Footwork

While some of the young fashion mavens wore old army boots with their jeans, others found designer boots by Beth and Herbert Levine more to their liking. In the sixties and seventies the Levines designed elegant see-through vinyl pumps and practical loafers. Their glamorous boots, both short and long, were made for walking, and were as high-fashion then as they are now.

The interest in collecting 60s and 70s fashions, along with those of earlier times, has brought private collections to auction. William Doyle Galleries and the Christie's auction of the Tina Chow collection included many pieces from these decades. All of which helps to establish some realistic prices and gives collectors guidelines for the designers and fashions to hunt down.

Clothing prices, unless noted otherwise, reflect auction prices.

For more detailed information on important designers and styles, see the listings in the bibliography and sources sections. Fashion is a subject that can be touched only briefly in a book such as this. The work of some obviously collectible designers might have been left out simply because there are no established prices available.

❋ INTERVIEW WITH MOLLY TURNER

The interest in vintage clothing began in the 60s as people rediscovered the past and reinvented vintage. I got interested in buying as a collector around that time. To me there is a mystique about the past. Clothing became seriously collectible in the late 70s with counterculture members digging through the trash for clothing and accessories. I started selling vintage items around that time. You know how it is. You start collecting, and before you know it there is no more room at home—so you begin to sell it. I began selling in the general shows and then the specialty shows with dolls and teddy bears. In 1984 I became a show promoter specializing in

FASHION MILESTONES

1965 Mary Quant, English designer who began in 1965, designed her first important collection; Biba, another English designer, also began work at this time.
British model Twiggy made thin the look for women.

1966–1967 Patterned hosiery in Op and Pop designs appeared, as did ankle boots with Pop designs.
Hats had exaggerated classical shapes, like the cloche.
Sunglasses assumed new importance and were often oversized and in new shapes, with bold optic motifs.
Jewelry, especially silver, used exaggerated geometric and asymmetrical shapes; in keeping with Pop Art, pieces were sometimes whimsical and humorous, for example one designer created a "double dip" ice cream brooch.
Acrylics were used for glamorous eveningwear shoes and purses by designers such as Judith Leiber.

Tip: Status symbol key rings were made by Gucci and others in Pop designs.

vintage clothing. We emphasized that these weren't just old clothes, but quality, clothing with a history.

There is a problem with fakes and reproductions. All my shows are vetted [checked by experts for reproductions]. Reproductions aren't acceptable, but restoration that doesn't basically alter a vintage piece is. An example of the latter would be altering the small "wasp waists" of an 1890s garment to fit a modern figure. It's not always easy to spot a new copy of an old "name" designer. Several years ago a dealer offered a vintage garment labeled "Chanel." A collector bought it and sent it to Chanel in Paris for some restoration. Unfortunately, they said it was unnumbered and not a Chanel garment at all. Of course, the dealer refunded the money. An exception to "new" would be decorator pillows made with old fabric.

Turner, who was an elementary school teacher before becoming a show promoter, has educated herself on the subjects of historical clothing and accessories. What does she collect for herself? "I collect old handmade laces and embroidery. It can't be duplicated if it is hand done. I don't mean the pattern-craft things offered in early magazines but the one-of-a-kind items." One of her prized vintage pieces is a sixteenth-century silver lace Flemish bonnet. "I found it in a shop in Chicago. You never know when something unique will turn up. I always ask the dealers in general merchandise shops if they have anything unusual. It was in a drawer, wrapped in acid-free paper tissue."

What should collectors be looking for if they want vintage items from the more recent past, say pieces from the 50s to the 70s? Her advice: "Get the most perfect and unique pieces. Condition relates to value. Museum people always look for offbeat things. And remember, the biggest dividend is enjoying what you buy. When buying these more contemporary pieces look for anything that speaks of the moment, of its design era. You have to develop a collector's eye."

As she pointed out, "trendy" is always overvalued. She cited the Lucite bags that were "super hot" a couple of years ago and, not surprisingly, overpriced. Now prices are leveling off.

❀ MENSWEAR ❀

The same changes that took place in women's fashions took place in men's clothing, and the change also began in London. However, unaccountably, men's clothing hasn't made it to the major vintage auctions and turns up mostly at collector's shows and in shops.

In London men's Mod boutiques sprang up not only on Carnaby Street but on King's Road as well. The variety was endless—from well-tailored suits in bold-colored sharkskin to

"Funky" Platform Shoes, late 1960s-early 1970s. Multi-color suede, men's shoes; $150. Courtesy of Have A Nice Day Shop.

Caftan, c. 1970. Cotton, "Dashiki," olive colored with African motif in maroon, rust, and yellow; $175. Courtesy of Harvey Hesse Collection.

shirts with Day-Glo graphics and rhinestones. Everything from Walt Disney characters to art by Max Ernst was used as design motifs.

Pierre Cardin launched a line of men's fashions in the early 60s that is often described as sculptural. The line included form fitting shirts and trousers, leather suits, and fur coats.

In the United States, turtleneck shirts replaced ties and button-down shirts as after-five evening wear. Ethnic was in, and everything from Moroccan caftans, American Indian fringed pants, and the African dashiki was the height of fashion.

Unisex fashions, interchangeable men's and women's fashions, were worn by both sexes.

❊ CLOTHING DESIGNERS ❊

CRISTOBAL BALENCIAGA (1895–1972)

This master couturier, who was best known for his fashion influence in the 1950s, continued working into the late 1960s. During his childhood in Spain, his mother, a seamstress, taught him to cut and sew. His first opportunity to design came when he was just a teenager and the Marquesa Casa de Torres financed his first trip to Paris and, later, his first tailoring shop. He became acquainted with the Paris couture in the 1920s with frequent trips to Paris as a buyer for a Spanish store. During this time he also opened his first two couture shops in Spain, both named Elsa.

After the death of Christian Dior in 1957, he became the ultimate haute couturier.

He was the first to use knee boots and tights in his couture in 1962. However, taste in fashions changed as it always does and he was forced to retire by 1967.

PRICES

Elsa Balenciaga Blouse (made from a Balenciaga scarf), c. 1962. Scarf of silk twill printed with a pattern of painterly large

---

Balenciaga Cocktail Dress, c. 1960s. Black, heavy silk slip dress with separate cape buttoning into the straps in back, no label; excellent condition; $1,000–1,500. Courtesy of William Doyle Auction Gallery.

white dots against a navy blue ground, label: Elsa and printed with the name Balenciaga; very good condition; $115.

Balenciaga Evening Dress and Overdress, mid-1960s. Bright lemon-yellow silk gazar with strapless, short underdress and curved long sleeveless cutaway overdress fastening with snaps and a self bow, label: 10 AVENUE GEORGE V, PARIS, together with a pair of matching pumps marked DESIGN BY EVINS; very good condition; $2,300/set.

Balenciaga Cocktail Dress, 1960s. Black heavy silk slip dress with separate cape buttoning to the straps in back; no label; excellent condition; $1,265.

Balenciaga Evening Coat, c. 1960. Candy-pink satin with notched lapel collar and four patch pockets with flaps, back with gathered yoke, label: BALENCIAGA 10 AVENUE GEORGE V, PARIS; very good condition; $1,150.

André Courrèges (1923–)

This fashion designer apprenticed with Cristobal Balenciaga from 1948 to 1959 in Paris. In 1961 he founded his own fashion house in the same city. He is best known for his minidresses, introduced in 1962, and the high-fashion Couture Future line of 1963. "Clothes," he once said, "must be liberating—they must escape convention." He was one of the designers who epitomized the spirit of youth with his "little girl look" for women. Because of the proliferation of copycat designs he divided his work into two lines. One was ready-to-wear and the other was the higher priced couture. In the late 60s he changed his approach, opting for body-hugging, figure-accentuating designs that were the forerunners of the bodysuits of today.

PRICES

Silver Lace Minidress and Lamé Coat, c. 1965. Silver organza woven with silver circles with keyhole-back neckline; label reads "COURREGES, PARIS"; together with a silver lamé coat; excellent condition; $575/set.

Baby Girl Dress and Jacket Ensemble, c. 1967. Ivory wool twill trimmed with embroidered navy wool scallops; label reads "COURREGES, PARIS"; very good condition; $431/set.

Leopard Suit, mid-1960s. Leopard wool; trimmed at the collar and cuffs with brown yarn fringe; label reads "COURREGES, PARIS"; excellent condition; $431.

Rudi Gernreich (1922–)

In 1938 Rudi Gernreich emigrated to the United States from his native Austria and became a naturalized citizen in 1943. After studying at Los Angeles City College (1938–1941), and the Los Angeles Art Center School (1941–1942), he held a variety of jobs before becoming a free-lance clothing designer. He worked in both New York and Los Angeles. He came to prominence with his topless women's swimwear in the 60s. In the

1960s he designed everything from swimwear to home furnishings for Knoll International, New York.

Considered an important designer of women's clothing in the 1960s, he offered easy-care fabrics and casual designs. His clothing showcased the human body whether he clad it in a see-through blouse or didn't cover it at all, as he did with the topless swimsuit. Many of his most popular designs were knitted minis. He also designed unisex caftans.

PRICES

Two Orange-and-White Japanese Schoolgirl Jumpers, c. 1960. Labels read "RUDI GERNREICH"; $316.

Two Silk Minidresses, mid-1960s. One made of bittersweet silk and printed in an abstract Japanese pattern of black and red; the other divided into four sections of similar swirly Op Art print in lime green, hot pink, mauve, or orange against a cream background; no labels; good to fair condition; $258.

Evening Bloomers, c. 1968. Black satin with wide belt loops and wide black patent leather belt; label reads "RUDI GERNREICH"; belt marked "RUDI GERNREICH"; excellent condition; $258.

Minidress, c. 1968. Black satin with high turtleneck fastening with a heavy brass zipper all the way down the side of the neck and the sleeve and down the side seam; labels read "RUDI GERNREICH and "MADE IN THE U.S.A."; excellent condition; $345.

Minidress, c. 1960s. Black and silver Lurex with bra top, fitted midriff, and flared skirt; label reads "RUDI GERNREICH DESIGN FOR HARMON KNITWEAR"; $86.

Dinner Dress, c. 1972. Navy wool knit; the bodice of navy wool ribbed knit with zipper front and short sleeves, the back and sleeves of transparent navy blue silk, the belt of navy blue knit with silvertone brass military slide buckle; no label; excellent condition; $1,725.

Paco Rabanne (1934–)

Fashion designer Paco Rabanne was born in Spain and emigrated to France in 1939. He was educated at the College of Morlaix, France, from 1940 to 1945 and studied architecture at the Ecole Nationale Superieure des Beaux-Arts in Paris from 1952 to 1964. From 1960 to 1964 he was a designer of accessories for such fashion houses as Givenchy and Christian Dior in Paris. As a free-lance fashion designer he began working in plastics, paper, and metal from 1965. In 1967 he established the Paco Rabanne fashion house and in 1981 the Maison Paco Rabanne furnishings company, both in Paris. He is best known today for his haute couture designs using the new materials of plastic, aluminium, and paper. Production often involved welding and molding these "wearable sculptures." In fact, a Paris art gallery showed his first designs, made of plastic and feathers, as Pop sculptures. It was his designs that made plastic and synthetics acceptable materials for fine clothing and jewelry.

PRICES

Paco Rabanne-Style Evening Coat, 1960s. Flat silver and black metal disks; very good condition; $460.

❈ Other Clothing Designers ❈

Note: These designs are listed alphabetically by designer. Uncredited pieces appear at the end of the section.

PRICES

Pair of Biba Leopard-Printed Lurex Bell-bottoms, c. 1970. Label reads "BIBA"; $373.

Pierre Cardin Boutique Day Dress, mid-1960s. Navy wool with pairs of inset seams descending from a yoke seam to form,

---

near the hem, paddle-shaped flaps lined in ivory wool; label reads "PIERRE CARDIN PARIS NEW YORK"; excellent condition; $3,680.

Chanel Suit, c. 1965. Ivory bouclé trimmed with navy flat wool braid and cerise knitted braid trim with gilt metal lion's head buttons and knitted cerise wool shell; label reads "CHANEL"; excellent condition; $805.

Sybil Connolly Cocktail Dress, c. 1960. Black pleated linen trimmed with black satin piping; label reads "SYBIL CONNOLLY DUBLIN"; excellent condition; $143.

Christian Dior Boutique At-Home Dress, c. 1960. Robin's-egg-blue silk faille with round neck, three-quarter-length sleeves, and buttoning down the front with self-covered buttons and bound buttonholes; self-belt; label reads "BOUTIQUE CHRISTIAN DIOR 1975"; excellent condition; $402.

Christian Dior Coat and Dress, 1971. White wool trimmed with white crocheted wool braid to resemble a djellaba; label reads "PRINTEMP-ETE, 1970 CHRISTIAN DIOR PARIS 151646"; very good condition; $230.

Christian Dior Ball Gown, c. 1961. White faille with Cleopatra collar bodice heavily embroidered with large curved pearlescent horsehair ornaments, pearls, rhinestones, silver thread, and crystal bugles; with sash of pink satin ribbon; label reads "CHRISTIAN DIOR AUTOMNE-HIVER 1961 PARIS 1656"; excellent condition; $1,265.

Christian Dior Suit, c. 1971. Double-faced herringbone wool in pink and white and black and white, the pink showing at notched lapel collar of the jacket; label reads "CHRISTIAN DIOR, PARIS, AUTOMNE-HIVER, 1971, 155972"; excellent condition; $287.

Galanos One-Shouldered Evening Dress, 1970s. Red silk worked with tambour-outlined trapunto; label reads "GALANOS"; very good condition; $373.

Galanos Cocktail Dress, c. 1960. Cinnamon silk chiffon; made as a sheer cape falling from the scooped front and back neckline to the hem of the narrow, sleeveless dress underneath;

the dress with cummerbund sash, the cape with arm slits; labels read "GALANOS" and "BONWIT TELLER"; very good condition; $172.

Givenchy Cocktail Dress and Stole, c. 1961. Black velvet edged with bands of black satin; the dress with camisole bodice, narrow skirt flared at the hem; the stole a long rectangle; label reads "GIVENCHY, MADE IN FRANCE 61.155"; very good condition; $517.

Givenchy Boutique Tiger-Stenciled Pony Vest and Skirt, 1960s. Excellent condition, except hem is let out; $172.

Gres Baby Blue Vinyl Evening Coat, 1960s. Lined with white knit and trimmed with white mink; very good condition; $258.

Gres Coral Qina At-Home Outfit, c. 1971. Tunic with boat neck; vertically tucked midriff and hem slanting from left knee to right ankle of the wearer; the pajama pants with straight legs; label reads "GRES, PARIS"; excellent condition; $373.

Guy Laroche Suede Evening Pantsuit, 1960s. Cardigan jacket and flared pants of caramel suede embroidered in gold and bronze in a passementerie pattern; label reads "GUY LAROCHE, PARIS"; very good condition; $258.

Guy Laroche Black Velvet Smoking Jacket, with two pairs of pants, 1960s. Short jacket with black moire lapels; one pair of pants ending in spats; label reads "GUY LAROCHE, PARIS, 512"; excellent condition; $460.

Mainbocher Coat, c. 1960. Oatmeal tweed with wide Peter Pan collar with self-tying bow and gathered skirt; label reads "MAINBOCHER INC."; very good condition; $460.

Mainbocher Rain Suit, c. 1960. Beige poplin lined in beige cashmere knit; the boxy jacket with flat collar; the dress with poplin skirt and cashmere top; label reads "MAINBOCHER INC."; very good condition; $172.

Mainbocher Eveningwear mix 'n match set, c. 1961. Candy-pink brocade long dress with draped camisole bodice and long stole; theater ensemble of lime-green tweed jacket lined in pink brocade; sleeveless dress with brocade bodice and tweed skirt and brocade ruff; label reads "MAINBOCHER INC."; very good condition; $460/set.

Jewelled Tunic Dress, by George Halley, c. 1960s. Black and cream ribbed wool embroidered with round and marquise rhinestones, label reads GEORGE HALLEY NEW YORK; *good condition; (not pictured, but included with the lot price, a pair of Beth Levine stocking boots with rhinestone-studded heels); $600–900.* Courtesy of William Doyle Auction Gallery.

Mainbocher Evening Coat, c. 1960. Lavender wild silk lined in lime-green wild silk; label reads "MAINBOCHER, INC."; very good condition; $287.

Mainbocher Cocktail Dress, c. 1960. Silver, bright blue, emerald-green, and yellow brocade; label reads "MAINBOCHER INC."; very good condition; $230.

Mainbocher Fur Suit, c. 1965. Cream broadtail with boxy short jacket and slightly flared skirt; label reads "MAINBOCHER INC. FOURRURES"; excellent condition; $345.

Maribou Evening Coat, 1960s. White floor-length cardigan coat lined with white silk printed with large red poppies, purple tulips, and lime-green leaves; very good condition; $345.

Norell Coat, 1960s. Beige wool with wide notched lapel collar of sable; label reads "NORMAN NORELL NEW YORK"; excellent condition; $287.

Norman Norell Empire Evening Dress, 1960s. Black wool crepe, sleeveless, with wide square neckline, high waist, wide black satin ribbon sash, and long slightly gathered skirt with scalloped hem; label reads "NORMAN NORELL FOR BONWIT TELLER"; has ILGWU tag; excellent condition; $230.

Norell Evening Ensemble, 1960s. Black wool jumpsuit and cardigan jacket trimmed with bands of rhinestones; labels read "NORMAN NORELL NEW YORK" and "SAKS FIFTH AVENUE"; $345.

Pucci-Printed Velvet Evening Suit, 1960s. Cardigan jacket and long sleeves printed in shades of emerald, lime green, magenta, and candy pink; label reads "EMILIO PUCCI FLORENCE-ITALY"; excellent condition; $172.

Yves Saint Laurent Beaded Minidress, c. 1967. Ivory organdy over pale peach silk; heavily embroidered with shaped geometric pearlized and silver plastic pieces surrounded by rhinestones, silver thread, and crystal beads; no label; excellent condition; $6,670.

Emmanuel Ungaro Boutique Ensemble, c. 1970. Eisenhower jacket and skirt of black and white striped and dotted wool; jersey blouse on white with black, red, and white handkerchief in jacket pocket; label reads "EMMANUEL UNGARO PARALLELE, PARIS"; very good condition; $287.

Uncredited Listings

Beaded Long Dress, 1960s. Ivory organza entirely covered with squares of bright geometric patterns in wool, pearls, rhinestones, and shaped sequins; good condition; $115.

Lamé Evening Dress, late 1960s. Printed in shades of tangerine, black, and silver and embroidered with black and gold shaped paillettes; very good condition; $115.

Hats

Adolfo Hat, 1960s. Zebra-striped haired calf kerchief hat

Clutch Purse, late 1960s. Plasticized French Elegance *magazine cover, over bentwood; $20.* Courtesy of The Time Machine.

with self-covered button; label reads "ADOLFO"; very good condition; $69.

Emme Jeweled Evening Hat, 1960s. Black net sewn with black and clear rhinestones and gold faceted beads; very good condition; $103.

Madcaps Black Patent Leather Tall Pillbox Hat, early 1960s. Label reads "ORIGINAL DESIGN BY MADCAPS, PARIS AND NEW YORK"; very good condition; $23.

White Deep Kid Pillbox, 1960s. Very good condition; $34.

Purses

Gucci Bamboo-Handled Pocketbook, 1960s. Brown pebble-grained leather with bamboo catch; marked "MADE IN ITALY BY GUCCI"; $172.

Koret Alligator Small Pocketbook, 1960s. Marked "KORET" and "MADE OF GENUINE ALLIGATOR"; very good condition; $373.

Judith Leiber Pocketbook, 1960s. Pearlized pewter leather in the shape of a treasure chest ornamented around the edges with silver studs; marked "JUDITH LEIBER"; excellent condition; $316.

Shawls and Scarves

Balenciaga Scarf, 1960s. Printed with Abstract Expressionist landscape in olive drab, emerald green, and cream with a fuchsia border; self-fringed edges; signed "BALENCIAGA, 100% SILK"; label reads "MADE IN FRANCE"; excellent condition except for some spots; $172.

Geoffrey Beene Scarves (two), 1960s. One made of silk twill printed with a large triangle pattern in spicy mustard, cream, and navy, self-fringed edges, labels read "GEOFFREY BEENE" and "MADE IN FRANCE"; the other limeade-green and lemon-yellow printed with an abstract pattern resembling the fanned-out pages of a book open at right angle, self-fringed edges, labels read "GEOFFREY BEENE" and "MADE IN FRANCE"; excellent condition; $46/set.

Hermes Scarf, 1970s. Titled *Frontaux et Cocardes;* printed in shades of gray, yellow-gold, beige, and brown; labels read "HERMES, PARIS, 100% SILK"; and "MADE IN FRANCE EXCLUSIVELY FOR BONWIT TELLER"; excellent condition; $230.

Twelve Evening Shawls, 1950s–1960s. Long, rectangular, self-fringe-edged satin shawls in turquoise, marigold, hot pink, candy pink, and cream; cream satin unfringed rectangle; rectangle of black wool jersey; cream satin and black taffeta rectangle trimmed with black velvet; three shawls of faille in royal blue, red, and candy pink; rose silk shawl; very good condition; $402/set.

BETH LEVINE

After working as a secretary and a shoe model, Beth Levine found her true calling as a shoe designer. After World War II she met and married Herbert Levine, and in 1948 they went into business together, forming one of the most innovative and influential partnerships in the history of shoe design. Their work is remarkable for both its quality and its inventiveness. Their most noteworthy creations include the stocking shoe, the extremely pointed toe, Lucite heels, see-through vinyl shoes, and the stretch boot.

PRICES

Levine Ankle Boots, 1960s. Chartreuse suede with red and white shaped wedge soles; marked "BETH'S BOOTERY"; very good condition; never worn; $690.

Levine Patchwork Ankle Boots, 1960s. Taupe velvet appliquéd with printed satin quilted flowers outlined in grass-green blanket stitch; marked "BETH'S BOOTERY"; good condition; $373.

Levine Black Satin Mongolian Boots with White Wedge Platform, 1960s. Marked "HERBERT LEVINE"; excellent condition; never worn; $575.

Levine Short Cut Booties, c. 1960. Bordeaux kid fastening up the sides with twelve oval buckles; very good condition; never worn; $115.

Levine Silver Skating Boots, 1960s. Silver calf trimmed with white mink; sprinkled with rhinestones; good condition; never worn; $437.

Levine Orange-and-Mauve Paper Mules, 1960s. Marked "HERBERT LEVINE"; excellent condition; never worn; $316.

Platform Pumps. Tortoise plastic; $30.

Levine "Caesar's Wife" Sandals, 1960s. With rhinestone studs; gladiator-style knee-high sandals of black suede ornamented with small rhinestones; marked "HERBERT LEVINE"; very good condition; $375.

Levine Brightly Striped Paper Sandals, 1960s. Marked "HERBERT LEVINE"; good condition; never worn; $575.

Pair of "Barefoot in the Grass" Shoes, 1960s. Astroturf and clear vinyl; good condition; some wear to one heel; $975.

Beth Racing Car Shoes, 1960s. Clear vinyl appliqués with racing car motifs; includes the name Beth with windshield wiper and windshield with shaped black suede soles; label says "HERBERT LEVINE"; very good condition; *note:* the renowned car shoes of Beth Levine for Herbert Levine were inspired by a quote from Marshall McLuhan's *The Medium Is the Message:* ". . . the foot is an extension of the wheel"; $316.

Levine Black Patent Leather Shoes, c. 1962. With shaped soles; marked "HERBERT LEVINE"; very good condition; $1,035.

Levine "Chinese Lantern Little Girl" Boots, 1960s. Red suede with slits from ankle to knee; excellent condition; $143.

Levine Speckled Leather Kabuki Shoes, c. 1962. Red and black shaped soles; label reads "KABUKI HERBERT LEVINE, 1962 PATENT PENDING"; very good condition; never worn; $402.

Fishnet Stocking Shoes, 1950s. Black satin high-heeled low-cut pumps with attached black fishnet seamed stockings; label reads "HERBERT LEVINE FINE SHOES"; excellent condition; *note:* this is the first pair of stocking shoes Beth Levine designed; $690.

Levine Silver Mesh Stocking Shoes, 1960s. With clear Lucite heels; marked "HERBERT LEVINE"; very good condition; never worn; $546.

Flatware

by
Jerryll Habegger

*A practicing designer and lecturer at the Harrington Insti-
tute of Design in Chicago, Illinois, Jerryll Habegger has
written not only about Modern flatware but also about Modern furniture, architecture, and plastic dinnerware. He has
been responsible for design concepts for some of Chicago's
most important buildings and has contributed similarly to
buildings in Europe. He is also a professional affiliate of
the American Institute of Architects and an active member
of the Society of Architectural Historians.*

The pleasures found in collecting Modern flatware are based
on an understanding of silver and stainless steel as materials.
Stainless steel's hard nature makes it a difficult material to
work, resulting in simpler designs. The totally three-
dimensional Rosebud ornament of traditional silver patterns
would be impossible to imprint into this tougher steel. Silver
is a more malleable material than stainless steel, thus designs
in silver can be more completely three-dimensional—that is to
say, with undercuts that are executed by hand, not by machine.

Beauty is found in the simplicity of Modern flatware. The
plain object requires a far greater degree of skill in its design
and fabrication than does the ornate object. Ornate complexity
hides all manner of defects.

Desirable qualities in Modern flatware include a strong visual expression, a heavier physical weight, and quality workmanship. Modern detailing achieves ornament through the
modeling of the basic form. In the manufacturing process, hot
stainless steel bars are beaten, or forged, into a die by a drop
hammer to change both their form and the thickness of a section. Variations within the material's thickness contribute to a
strong expression and a heavier visual weight. On fine-quality
pieces, over 50 percent of the operations for manufacturing
and the achievement of a fine finish are done by hand.

❀ COMPOSITION OF SILVER AND STAINLESS STEEL FLATWARE

Sterling silver, the most costly of these flatware materials, is
925 parts silver, 75 parts copper, and is marked "925" or "ster-

ling." Silver is composed of 800 parts pure silver, 200 parts copper, and is marked "800" or "silver." Silver plate is made of 90 grams of silver over alpaca (copper, zinc, and nickel alloy), and is marked "plated." Stainless steel is made of 74 percent iron, 18 percent chromium, 8 percent nickel alloy, and is marked "18/8" or "18/10."

In the presence of moisture, the stronger metal alloys will corrode the weaker alloys. Corrosion may also occur with exposure to the following solutions: well water with a high iron content; oxalic acid found in rhubarb; and acids found in mustard, vinegar, lemon juice, and salt.

❀ CHARACTERISTICS OF MODERN FLATWARE

Modern eating habits have dictated food that is smaller in size and softer in consistency. Knife blades have become smaller, however, with a greater curve. The shorter tines of the fork fit the smaller food quantities and the smaller elliptically shaped bowl of the spoon passes easily through the mouth. In many patterns, all of the utensils are of the same length and are balanced for good weight distribution in the hand. Another characteristic of Modern flatware is the one-piece (nonhollow) handle. It is often given greater width at the center to afford a better grip and greater comfort in handling. Additionally, the handles on some of the patterns allow pieces to be stacked.

❀ POPULAR FLATWARE PATTERNS

The designers of the 1950s advanced Modern flatware with tapered forms and soft organic curves, whereas bolder, more experimental forms became characteristic of the 1960s and 1970s. Specifically, in the 1960s greater dimensional variation was given to the thicknesses of the handle. Examples are the patterns Jette and Prism. Additionally, the entire form became more abstracted, as expressed in the Composition pattern. In the 1970s the handle shape became more exaggerated in scale. Examples are Mango, with a large spread, and Instrumenta, with a very thin wrap. The following are representative of this time period.

In 1964 Alexander Schaffner designed the "89" pattern sterling silver for Pott. The spoon and fork of this pattern utilize strong geometric shapes: the bowl of the fork is wide and angular and the bowl of the spoon is a broad circular shape. The wide knife blade is a soft organic curve and is perpendicular to the handle. This pattern is still in production. This is the type of design that was commonly knocked off in stainless steel by the Japanese during the 60s and 70s. The Japanese did not really pursue their own original designs for flatware until the early 80s.

Flatware, design 89, by Alexander Schaffner, c. 1964. Sterling silver, 3 pieces.

Flatware, designed by Carlo Scarpa for the Cleto Munari Collection of Italy, produced by Rossi & Arcandi. Sterling silver, 7 pieces show for detailing.

Large teaspoon	$170
Dinner fork	$170
Dinner knife	$125

In 1977, Carlo Scarpa designed flatware in sterling silver for the Cleto Munari Collection of Italy. This is produced by Rossi and Arcandi. Carlo Scarpa is known for his attention to detail in his architectural works. In this pattern the handle is notched so that one can rest the utensil on the edge of a plate or bowl. From the notch, two lines extend toward and surround the bowls. On the knife, the two lines extend downward to define the handle as separate from the blade. The fork has five tines. The pattern is still in production.

Large teaspoon	$230
Dinner fork	$220
Dinner knife	$175

Flatware, design Jette, c. 1960. Stainless steel, designed by Jens Quistgaard for Dansk.

Jette is one of many stainless steel patterns designed by Jens Quistgaard in 1960 for Dansk. Unique to Jette is the flared rod handle wrapped with concentric circles for easy grip. The bowl on the spoon is a large, round shape, whereas the tines and blades are elongated. The bowls and blades are defined with an edge that is an extension of the handle. This pattern is out of production.

Large teaspoon	$25
Dinner fork	$25
Dinner knife	$25

In 1961, Tapio Wirkkala designed the stainless steel Composition for Rosenthal. He is considered to be one of the preeminent twentieth-century craftsmen. The form of the Composition knife is a radical departure from traditional cutlery. The act of cutting suggests that the forefinger is placed

Flatware, design Composition, c. 1961. Stainless steel, designed by Tapio Wirkkala for Rosenthal, 3 pieces.

on top of the blade. In this design the blade is dropped down below the handle to accommodate the forefinger. This pattern is still in production.

Large teaspoon	$27
Dinner fork	$27
Dinner knife	$34

Tias Eckhoff designed Maya in stainless steel in 1961 for Norsk Stalpress. The design is a balanced composition between elongated and rounded forms. The two-dimensional graphic quality of the pattern expresses a strong clarity of purpose and sense of touch. The pieces are large in scale and are still in production.

Large teaspoon	$18
Dinner fork	$18
Dinner knife	$26

Flatware, design Maya, c. 1961. Stainless steel, designed by Tias Eckhoff for Norsk Stalpress.

Flatware, design Prism, c. 1962. Stainless steel, designed by Gert Holbek and Jorgen Dahlerup for Georg Jensen, 3 pieces.

Gert Holbek and Jorgen Dahlerup designed Prism in stainless steel in 1962 for Georg Jensen. Prism gives an illusion of an extreme taper. The blade and bowl edges taper down through the handle to create a prismatic shape at the end. A very thin handle is expressed with the gripping advantage of a heavier handle. The angular quality of the handle is beautifully articulated in the sculptural cake serving piece. This pattern is still in production.

Large teaspoon	$19
Dinner fork	$26
Dinner knife	$30

Don Wallance was the predominant American designer of sculptural flatware in the 60s and 70s. One of his best designs

Flatware, design Design 3, c. 1963. Stainless steel, designed by Don Wallance for Lauffer, 3 pieces.

is the 1963 stainless steel pattern Design 3 for Lauffer. This pattern is thinner than his previous designs. It is also totally unified in detail—and to the touch, well balanced. This pattern is no longer in production.

Large teaspoon	$12
Dinner fork	$15
Dinner knife	$15

In 1965, Svend Siune designed Blue Shark. This stainless steel design was an offspring of the competition celebrating the centenary of Georg Jensen's birth. All the pieces of this pattern are plain sculptural forms and have very strong interrelationships. The pieces are matte in finish, seamless, and heavy in weight, providing a pleasing tactile experience. This pattern is still in production.

Flatware, design Blue Shark, c. 1965. Stainless steel, designed by Svend Siune for Georg Jensen, 3 pieces.

Flatware, design 2729, c. 1967. Stainless steel, designed by Hans Schweippert for Pott, 3 pieces.

Large teaspoon	$13
Dinner fork	$15
Dinner knife	$28

In 1967, Hans Schweippert designed the "2729" place setting in stainless steel of very bold forms for Pott. This pattern is composed of only five pieces: two dinner forks, one with longer tines, the other with a bowl and multiple short tines; one very dramatic organically shaped dinner knife; one large-bowled dinner spoon; and one teaspoon with implied tines. This pattern is still in production.

Large teaspoon	$13
Dinner fork	$16
Dinner knife	$28

In 1970, Joe Colombo and Ambrogio Pozzi designed the Alitalia pattern, which was manufactured in stainless steel by Pinti of Italy. This series evolved from a study of objects for use on aircraft. Stackability is a requirement for compact storage; the pieces are very broad and flat, thus easily stacked. Safety is a requirement in case of heavy turbulence; the flatware has soft rounded edges so that pieces will not become dangerous if tossed around in the cabin. This pattern is still in use, along with a design in plastic by the same designers.

Large teaspoon	$12
Dinner fork	$12
Dinner knife	$12

In 1978, Lino Sabattini designed the Instrumenta pattern in stainless steel for Zani and Zani of Italy. Instrumenta is a wonderful example of an inexpensive flatware series that has

Flatware, design Alitalia, c. 1970. Stainless steel, designed by Joe Colombo and Ambrogio Pozzi for Pinti of Italy, 3 pieces.

Flatware, design Instrumenta, c. 1978. Stainless steel, designed by Lino Sabattini for Zani & Zani of Italy, 3 pieces.

extreme artistic form. It is industrially produced, but offers a dramatic handcrafted type of design for a broad audience. The folded-material concept of Russel Wright's Highlight knife of 1953 has been extended to a complete flatware series. This pattern is still in production.

Large teaspoon	$12
Dinner fork	$14
Dinner knife	$12

Gerald Gulotta designed the Chromatics pattern in 1971 in stainless steel for Block China. This pattern is an interesting interplay of flared and tapered handles. The dinner fork and spoon have tapered handles. In contrast, the dinner knife, salad fork, and dessert spoon are flared at the bottom in order to balance a wide blade shape or a wider bowl. This pattern is out of production.

Flatware, design Chromatics, c. 1971. Stainless steel, designed by Gerald Gulotta for Block China, 3 pieces.

Flatware, design Mango, c. 1972. Stainless steel, designed by Nanny Still McKinney for Hackmann of Finland, 3 pieces.

Large teaspoon	$10
Dinner fork	$10
Dinner knife	$10

Nanny Still McKinney designed the Mango pattern in stainless steel in 1972 for Hackmann of Finland. The Mango pattern is physically heavy. The silhouettes of the pieces are very dramatic. The dinner knife is delineated with one clear gracious shape for the cutting blade. The necks between the handles and the bowls and blades are elongated, clearly articulating the various parts. This pattern is still in production.

Large teaspoon	$10
Dinner fork	$11
Dinner knife	$12

* * *

Furniture Designers
and Manufacturers

❋ ❋ ❋ ❋ ❋

Writing about American and international designers can be a confusing task. The problem arises when trying to put them into an organized sequence. Many worked not only in their own studios but for other manufacturers as well. To add to the confusion, they were a creative lot who often designed in other media from glass to metals. Therefore, you will find objects and prices listed under the various manufacturers' names. There are separate entries in other sections for their glass, ceramic, and other designs.

The following listings are organized alphabetically.

Because many designers such as Charles Eames and Jens Risom were so prolific, it has been difficult to condense their backgrounds in the small space allotted. An extensive bibliography in the back of the book offers further information.

The same is true for architect Frank Lloyd Wright, whose life and work have been written about extensively. Examples of his work included in this book are furniture designs for mass (though relatively small) production.

❋ AMERICAN FURNITURE DESIGNERS ❋

ARIETO (HARRY) BERTOIA (1915–1978)

Like many of the designers who began working in the late 30s, Bertoia selected one medium—metal—and adapted it to furniture, jewelry, hollowware, and art. Born in Italy, he came to America in 1930 and received a scholarship to the Cranbrook Academy of Art. This was an important influence on the direction his work would take, since the school was combining the new industrial designs with the philosophy of the Arts and Crafts movement.

While there, Bertoia began teaching metalcraft and producing some of his own designs using the Streamlined style. The metal shortages of World War II closed the metalcraft department, and he was moved to the graphics department. During the 1940s he began doing monoprints, at first in the manner of Kandinsky and Klee; later they became more abstract. In 1943 he moved to California and began working with Charles and Ray Eames. After a short period Bertoia, whose primary interest was metal (including its use as part of furniture design), left the Eameses to work on his new concept of metal wire furniture.

It was Knoll Associates, of Pennsylvania, who produced his Diamond chair in 1953. Bertoia described it, and his other metal wire furniture, as "functional sculpture." The Diamond armchair, model 421-1, is still being made. The original models were made by hand. Early labels, printed in black on paper and attached to the cushion, read "KNOLL/KNOLL ASSOCIATES INC/ 320 PARK AVE. N.Y. (along with a stylized "K" printed in red). In spite of the success of his furniture designs, Bertoia expressed his disdain in the November 1965 issue of *Interiors*, saying, "Furniture is nothing to me—it was a means of eating."

WENDELL CASTLE (1932–   )

Castle was born in Emporia, Kansas, and received his B.F.A. and M.F.A. degrees from the University of Kansas in Lawrence in 1958 and 1961, respectively. He was a faculty member of the Rochester Institute of Technology in New York and SUNY Brockport. His works are in public collections at the Art Institute of Chicago; the Metropolitan Museum of Art, New York; the Museum of Fine Arts, Boston; the Museum of Modern Art, New York; the Philadelphia Museum of Art; the Smithsonian Museum of Art, Washington, D.C.; and the Museum of Applied Arts in Oslo, Norway.

> I feel my 60s work went into the 70s and was revolutionary work. It actually goes from 1958 to 1972. The molar chair came about as a missing link. In the 60s I began painting wood pieces in bright colors. But, being an organic material, it didn't work. But I wanted that look of a perfect glass automobile finish. The molar chair was initially done in white, but was also offered

in red, green, and other colors. In 1968 or 1969 I designed a dozen pieces for molded plastic production by the Balerian Company. Stendig did two of the designs as tables. They were in limited production, not to exceed 500 pieces overall.

In the 60s I also did some small things such as sculptured wall mirrors and jewelry boxes. Probably some have been imitated. Back in the 60s, when a New York store, America House, was in business, they displayed some forged work attributed to me. While there are pieces similar to mine, I haven't seen any with faked signatures.

At the Sotheby auction of contemporary

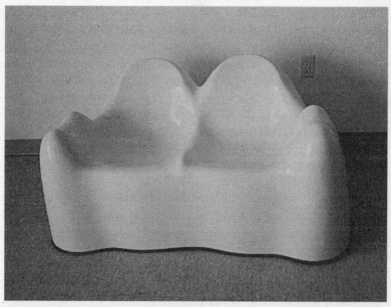

Double Molar Loveseat, designed by Wendell Castle, c. 1967. Part of a whimsical molar collection, white polyester reinforced plastic; $1500. Courtesy of Anthony Du Pont Collection.

Illusions Coat Rack, designed by Wendell Castle, 1978. Laminated and carved mahogany, signed and dated; 5 feet, 11½ inches high; $85,250. Courtesy of Wendell Castle.

works of art, in 1992, my pieces sold to private collectors. There are probably at least a thousand of my pieces that will begin coming to market. Of all my pieces I feel the coat rack and the Scribe's stool are among the most important. All of my work is signed with an arc monogram or initials.

I think of my furniture as sculpture. Most of it doesn't qualify as functional.

Advice to Collectors: Collectors should look for

the important names. Out of that 1992 Sotheby's auction, only my pieces and Dale Chihuly's glass really did well. In that auction there was a vanity offered based on one of my designs and wrongly attributed to me. Check exhibition catalogs and when a piece comes to auction that should have a signature, such as mine, and doesn't, chances are it is a fake.

PRICES

Chair, 1970s. Molar tooth form; white fiberglass; $5,000.

Wendell Castle Desk, Table, Six Chairs, and Storage Unit, 1976. Laminated and carved maple; signed and dated "76"; back section 35 inches high × 10 feet long; table section 29 inches high; $72,000.

Wendell Castle Teak Music Stand, 1969. Shaped music platform on tripod-shaped stand; signed and dated "w.c. 69" and numbered "NO. 11/12"; 34 inches high; $3,200.

DUNBAR FURNITURE CORPORATION OF INDIANA

This furniture company, founded in 1919, came to prominence when furniture designer Edward J. Wormley joined them in 1931. Their designs were Traditional until Wormley introduced pieces influenced by Swedish Modern. By the end of the 1930s the company manufactured both Traditional and Modern furniture. By 1957 the company had introduced its largest line: the 150-piece Janus collection. While the designs are for the most part conservative, they concentrated on fine craftsmanship and materials.

Many of the older Wormley pieces are still being made.

PRICES

Dunbar Shelving Unit, c. 1960s. Ivory lacquered wood cut in optical configuration with inset glass shelves; very unusual; 79 inches high × 20 inches square; excellent condition; $960.

CHARLES EAMES (1907–1978)
RAY KAISER EAMES (1913–1988)

Both Charles Eames and his wife, Ray, are important figures in modern American design. Their careers included not only furniture design, but also architecture, interior design, film-making, and exhibition design. Charles Eames began his study of architecture at Washington University in Saint Louis, Missouri. In 1938 he was awarded a fellowship to study architecture and design at Cranbrook Academy of Art in Bloomfield Hills, Michigan. His friendship with faculty member Eero Saarinen led to a joint project on modular furniture. The resultant molded plywood chair won them two first prizes in a competition sponsored by the Museum of Modern Art called "Organic Design in Home Furnishings." Ray Kaiser, a sculptor and artist, who assisted in the project, shortly became Eames's wife. They were lifelong collaborators. In 1946, the Eameses exhibited in a major show devoted to their works at the Museum of Modern Art. A series begun in 1949 introduced their furnishings in molded polyester. In 1958 they began another series, this time using aluminum. Their classic lounge chair and ottoman of aluminum, rosewood, and leather was exhibited in 1958.

Among Charles Eames's noteworthy pieces of the 1960s are:

- 675 lobby chair (1960) in cast aluminum with leather upholstery, for Herman Miller.

- LaFonda chair (1960) in cast aluminum and fiberglass, with polyfoam upholstery, for Herman Miller.

- Eames Contract Storage (1961) (cupboard/bed/study units) in birch plywood, for Herman Miller.

- RE-204 sofa (1962) in aluminum with polyfoam and plastic upholstery, for Herman Miller.

- Chaise ES106 (1969) (Soft Pad group) in aluminum with polyfoam and leather cushions, for Herman Miller.

During their long careers the husband-and-wife team produced some fifty films.

You can view examples of their work in Washington, D.C. In 1985 the Library of Congress, assisted by a grant of $500,000 from International Business Machines, established a large Eames archive that includes drawings, letters, films, and photographs.

PRICES

Charles Eames Chaise, manufactured by Herman Miller, Soft Pad group, c. 1960s. Black base of aluminum, six connected black leather cushions; 29 inches high × 79 inches long × 17 inches wide; excellent condition; $500.

Charles Eames LaFonda Chairs (pair), manufactured by Herman Miller, c. 1960s. Sculptural form of molded fiberglass upholstered in original forest-green Naugahyde with pedestal base of four separate elliptical chrome-plated steel rods that attach to base; 25 inches wide × 26 inches deep × 29 inches long; excellent condition; $450.

Charles Eames LaFonda Cocktail Table, manufactured by Herman Miller. Round slate top supported by pedestal base of four separate elliptical chrome-plated steel rods that attached to base; 17 inches high × 30 inches in diameter; excellent condition; $600.

Ray Eames Time Life Stool, manufactured by Herman Miller, c. 1960. Only version of the original four designed for the Time Life Building; no longer in production; original walnut finish; 15 inches high × 13 inches in diameter; excellent condition; $1,200.

FRANK GEHRY (1930–)

Raised in Toronto, Canada, Frank Gehry moved to Los Angeles in 1947. He received his Bachelor of Architecture degree from the University of Southern California and studied city planning at Harvard University's graduate school of design. In subsequent years he built an architecture career that has spanned three decades, producing public and private buildings in America, Japan, and, most recently, in Europe. In 1989 Gehry was awarded the premier accolade of the architectural field, the Pritzker Architecture Prize. In 1992 he received the Wolf Prize in Art, and has received many international awards. A trustee of the American Academy in Rome, he has taught at Yale and Harvard universities. A major retrospective exhibition, "The Architecture of Frank O. Gehry," was organized by the Walker Art Center in 1986 and traveled to the most important museums in the United States.

His design work included decorative and functional pieces. His Easy Edges furniture group made of laminated cardboard was a cutting-edge and low-cost solution to home decor. Though the line was immediately successful, Gehry, who held the patent, stopped production after only three months.

PRICES

Chairs/Stools

Easy Edges Laminated Cardboard Side Chair, designed by Frank Gehry, c. 1970. With slab leg and reverse cant; 32½ inches high × 19 inches deep × 16 inches wide; $920.

Nest of Three Laminated Cardboard Easy Edges Chairs, designed by Frank Gehry, c. 1972. Three scrolling seats of graduated size constructed of laminated corrugated cardboard with fiberboard ends; 29 inches high × 40 inches deep × 18 inches wide; $4,950/set.

Easy Edges Laminated Cardboard Side Chair, designed by Frank Gehry, c. 1972. Continuous back and compressed scroll base formed of laminated corrugated cardboard with fiber-

---

board ends; 33½ inches high × 23 inches deep × 14½ inches wide; $3,300.

Easy Edges Laminated Cardboard Stools and Console Table (pair), designed by Frank Gehry, c. 1972. Each of compressed scroll form and constructed of laminated corrugated cardboard sections with fiberboard ends; together with a console table of straight sides and flat top constructed in a similar manner; stools 16 inches high × 17 inches deep × 15¾ inches wide; console table 26 inches high × 14 inches deep × 60 inches wide; $11,000/set.

Easy Edges Laminated Cardboard Wiggle Chair and Footstool, designed by Frank Gehry, c. 1970. Base as a compressed scroll continuing to a canted back; 32½ inches high; matching stool 15¾ inches high; $1,725/set.

Frank Gehry Desk Chair, manufactured by Easy Edges, Inc., c. 1971. Sculptural geometric continuous form of laminated corrugated cardboard; 32 inches high × 20 inches deep × 16 inches wide; excellent condition; $900.

Frank Gehry Stool, manufactured by Easy Edges, Inc., c. 1971. Sculptural form of molded and laminated corrugated cardboard and Masonite; 15 inches high × 16 inches deep × 16 inches wide; very good condition; $500.

Frank Gehry Stool, manufactured by Easy Edges, Inc., c. 1971. Sculptural form of molded and laminated corrugated cardboard and Masonite; 15 inches high × 16 inches deep × 16 inches wide; very good condition; $55.

Desks/Tables

Frank Gehry Desk/Console, manufactured by Easy Edges, Inc., c. 1971. Rectangular form of natural laminated corrugated cardboard with fiberboard sides; 28 inches high × 14 inches deep × 60 inches wide; excellent condition; $700.

Frank Gehry Table, manufactured by Easy Edges, Inc., c. 1971. Hollow cube form of laminated corrugated cardboard; 17 inches high × 17 inches deep × 17 inches wide; excellent condition; $200.

Lamps

Easy Edges Laminated Cardboard Table Lamp, designed by Frank Gehry, c. 1972. Cylindrical base holding a conical shade; formed of corrugated cardboard with plywood ends; paper label; 26½ inches high; $690.

HEYWOOD-WAKEFIELD

While the name Heywood-Wakefield has been most closely associated with woven reed and bentwood furniture, it is the 40s–60s pieces that are appealing to budget-conscious Modern collectors. As early as the 1930s the company was influenced by the Scandinavian use of light woods, such as birch, and by the Modern look, popularized by the Swedish Exhibition held in London in 1930. In 1931 Heywood-Wakefield commissioned Gilbert Rohde, a New York industrial designer, to create some pieces in the new, light woods for mass production.

By the 1940s the company was offering the fashionable "blond" woods in styles similar to contemporary Scandinavian furniture. By the 1950s Modern light wood furnishings (many of them made by Heywood-Wakefield) had found their way to hotel rooms. This hotel room furniture, usually refinished, is coming to market today. Prices are modest compared with prices of other pieces of the period. Postwar pieces, both those sold retail and for hotel use, had a wood-burned stamp. Pieces that can be attributed to a name designer such as Russel Wright or Gilbert Rohde command higher prices.

PRICES

Heywood-Wakefield Triple Dresser (#M1529), c. 1964. Twelve drawers with softly curving drawer fronts, solid wood longitudinal pulls, full-width mirror; all solid hand-rubbed northern birch on four swivel caster wheels under recessed pedestal base; wheat finish; 68 inches high × 20 inches deep × 62 inches wide; excellent condition; $650.

Vladimir Kagan (1927–   ) A.S.I.D., A.S.F.D.

Kagan's career spans forty years of pioneering Modern design. Born in Worms am Rhein in Germany, he came to the United States in 1938 with his family. He studied architecture at Columbia University and joined his father's woodworking shop in 1947. His earliest success came with the design for the Delegate's Cocktail Lounges for the first United Nations headquarters in Lake Success, New York (1947–1948). In 1949 he opened a showroom in New York City. Over the years his company opened showrooms throughout America as the preeminent haute couture design and custom furniture manufacturing facility in the United States. At the end of those first forty years, Kagan closed his factory and showrooms to concentrate on his first love: designing.

In the 60s Kagan adapted many of his innovative designs to acrylic, often combining this material with rare woods. One of his most striking pieces is his crescent desk, designed in 1976.

"I used fiddleback olive ash for the top of the crescent desk, but a Plexiglas base," he said. It was "originally designed for a client, to be placed on a beautiful Oriental rug. The use of Plexiglas allowed the rug to be seen—solving a decorating problem."

When I had a chance I worked with architects. I could do details. I had my own factory, Kagan Designs, begun by my father. I began in 1939, when we came to America as refugees, as a cabinetmaker. The factory became a custom shop with pride in craftsmanship. Where the Eameses were concerned with industrial and machine-designed pieces, my motivation was craftsmanship. I began working with organic forms in 1947. I am best known for my innovative Modern designs that began in the early fifties with organic sculptural Modernism and

Crescent Desk, designed by Vladimir Kagan, c. 1970. Rosewood with modesty panel of walnut with ebony finish. Courtesy of Vladimir Kagan Design Group, Inc.

went on to explore the architectural minimalism of the sixties and seventies . . . and continued into the Postmodernism and Neoclassic designs of the eighties. I consider the 1956 rocking chair and the 1960s Unicorn chair two of my signature pieces. While many of my designs are being reproduced today, these two are out of production. Another innovation was my use of lights as an element in the late 1960s. I used both fluorescent and cold cathode.

Today, Kagan is creating designs inspired by the deconstructionist movement of the nineties tempered by a strong flair for the organic sculpturism that was his trademark in the fifties.

His works are in the permanent collections of the Brooklyn Museum, the Vitra Design Museum of Weil am Rhein in Germany, and the Cooper Hewitt Museum in Manhattan. His designs were originally shown in the Museum of Modern Art's "Good Design" exhibit in 1958 and were most recently shown, in 1991, at the London Design Museum's Organic Design Show. In 1980, New York's Fashion Institute of Technology (F.I.T.) honored Kagan with a thirty-year retrospective exhibit called "Three Decades of Design."

He has designed furniture for individual clients such as Marilyn Monroe, and acted as design consultant to such diversified clients as General Electric, Walt Disney, and the Kingdom of Saudi Arabia. A number of Kagan's pieces have been reproduced and copied over the years. Collectors should carefully examine the quality of workmanship, which is tops on original pieces. Study fabrics used in different periods versus contemporary ones and use quality as a basis of comparison when you suspect a piece is a cheap knock-off of the period. As Kagan points out, "the repros don't use the old upholstery techniques."

PRICES

Vladimir Kagan Sofa, c. 1960. Unusual biomorphic form with sculpted backrest resting on crisscrossed teak legs in original oatmeal Zulu Dreyfuss fabric; 28 inches high × 30 inches deep × 90 inches wide; very good condition; minor fading to lower back; $3,000.

KNOLL ASSOCIATES

Founded in 1938 by Hans Knoll, this company was an international furniture manufacturer and distributor specializing in Modernist furniture. Over the following decades some of the world's foremost architects and designers worked for the com-

---

Desk Chair, designed by Vladimir Kagan, c. 1969. Plexi desk chair-channel back, molded polyfoam and hair on rubber spring, mirror finish cast aluminum swivel tilt base and casters, clear plexi shell (also bronze, black, or white), fabric vinyl or leather; 29 inches high × 24 inches deep × 21 inches wide. Courtesy Vladimir Kagan Design Group Inc.

pany. Hans Knoll came to America from Germany in 1937. He started the Hans C. Knoll Furniture Company in New York City, hiring another new arrival, Jens Risom, from Denmark. In 1941 Risom designed Knoll's first chair, establishing the simplistic style that would define the Knoll look.

Florence Shust married Hans Knoll in 1941 and became an important part of the company. She was a graduate of the Cranbrook Academy of Art and had previously worked for Walter Gropius and Marcel Breuer.

The impressive roster of designers who worked for Knoll over the years includes Isamu Noguchi, Eero Saarinen, and Harry Bertoia. The firm opened a textile division in 1947, utilizing the talents of such well-known talents as Marianne Stengell and, later, Eszter Haraszty.

Upon the death of Hans Knoll, Florence Knoll assumed the presidency of the company. Four years later the firm was sold to Art Metal, which manufactured traditional metal office furniture.

In 1969, after ownership changed hands more than once, the company's name was changed to Knoll International. In 1977 General Felt Industries took over. The firm is currently owned by one of the partners of General Felt, Marshall S. Cogan.

PRICES

Florence Knoll Credenza, manufactured by Knoll International, c. 1950. Simple architectural form of teak consisting of eight regular drawers and two large drawers floating on chrome-plated steel frame; topped with white Carrara marble; 25 inches high × 18 inches deep × 75 inches wide; very good condition; minor chip to marble in back; $1,600.

Florence Knoll Desk Organizer, c. 1960. Composed of two ebonized molded plywood trays conjoined by an aluminum pin; retains paper labels; 7¾ inches high × 15 inches long × 11½ inches wide; $690.

Warren Platner Console Table/Desk, manufactured by Knoll, c. 1960s. Walnut-and-leather top; bronze base; three floating planes compose the simple construction; Knoll tags; 30 inches high × 32 inches deep × 60 inches wide; very good condition; $1,000.

RAYMOND LOEWY (1893–1986)

Though this famous designer achieved fame initially in the 1930s, his long career continued well into the 1960s. He attended both the Université de Paris and the École de Laneau in his native France, where he received a degree in engineering. He immigrated to New York in 1919, and by 1929 he had opened his own industrial design firm. He designed everything from the famous bullet-shaped Pennsylvania Railroad S-1 locomo-

*Dining Room Set (chair shown), designed by Warren Platner,
manufactured by Knoll Associates, c. 1970. Sculptural forms of vertical
steel wire rods welded to circular horizontal and edge framing rods,
smoked-glass table top, four chairs upholstered in teal blue Knoll fabric;
chairs measure 29 inches high × 20 inches deep × 27 inches wide, table
measures 28 inches high × 50 inches in diameter; $1,600.* Courtesy of
Toomey-Treadway Galleries, Oak Park, IL.

tive (1937) to furniture. More detailed information on his
achievements can be found in many other books.

Over the years he established many firms in the United
States and other countries. Always in touch with the times, he
designed furniture using newly developed materials such as
plastics, popular in 1968.

HERMAN MILLER FURNITURE COMPANY
The Herman Miller Company has been well known since the
1940s as one of the leading manufacturers of Modern furniture
in the United States. Under the direction of design consultant
George Nelson (see the following listing under his name), be-

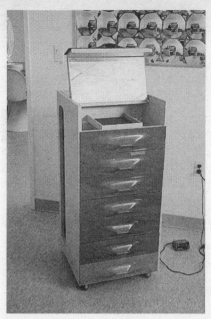

Mirrored Men's Wardrobe and Toiletry Kit, designed by Raymond Loewy, manufactured by CEI of Paris, c. 1968. Part of a set designed for the DF 2000 series, white painted wood with reinforced plastic and fiberglass drawers; 39 inches high × 20 inches wide × 20 inches deep; $750. Courtesy of Anthony Du Pont Collection.

ginning in 1946, the company concentrated on producing pieces from Modern-oriented designers such as Isamu Noguchi and Charles and Ray Eames.

In 1970 Alexander Girard joined the textile and wallpaper division as a designer, bringing his geometric fabrics to the company's furniture. Important designers who worked there in the 60s and 70s included Poul Kjaerholm, Fritz Haller, and Verner Panton.

PRICES

Drafter's Perch, designed by Robert Probst, Action Office Group, c. 1964. Animated form of polished aluminum chrome-

---

Side Chairs, designed by Verner Panton, produced by Vitra GmbH for Herman Miller International, 1968–1979; $500 each (dealer price). Sculptured, Luran-S thermoplastic, (also shown dining table by Isamu Noguchi, c. 1953); chairs $467. Courtesy of Treadway Gallery.

plated steel and black Naugahyde; upholstered seat and back; 40 inches high × 10 inches deep × 19 inches wide; excellent condition; $700.

Verner Panton/Herman Miller Chairs (four), c. 1960. Four stacking chairs; reinforced polyester and molded fiberglass; one-piece continuous form; two are white, one green, one orange, 33 inches high × 23 inches deep × 29 inches wide; excellent condition; $425/set.

GEORGE NAKASHIMA (1905–1990)

George Nakashima graduated with a bachelor's degree in architecture from the University of Washington in Seattle in 1929. He later earned a master's degree in architecture from the Massachusetts Institute of Technology in 1930. His works are included in the collections of the Museum of Fine Arts in Boston, the Philadelphia Museum of Art, the American Craft Museum in New York, and the Victoria and Albert Museum in London.

PRICES

Tables

George Nakashima Dining Room Table. Rectangular top with free edges joined through the center with three butterfly keys; on a trestle base with oval stretcher; with two free-edged extension leaves; 29 inches high × 41¾ inches deep × 60 inches wide; leaves measure 14 inches wide; $2,990.

George Nakashima Walnut Coffee Table, c. 1960. Irregular thick top raised on four shaped turned legs; 13½ inches high × 75 inches long × 26 inches wide; $2,300.

George Nakashima Walnut Conoid Dining Table and Six New Dining Chairs, c. 1965. Table with dovetail rectangular top with two extensions; raised on angled legs on a trestle base; each chair with elliptical crest rail above slightly swelling spindles, shaped seat raised on tapering cylindrical legs joined by stretchers; table 29 inches high × 84 inches long; $4,000.

Chairs/Benches

George Nakashima Walnut Long Bench. Elongated rectangle with free edge on five tapering legs; 14¼ inches high × 22½ inches deep × 133 inches wide; $1,495.

Six George Nakashima New Chairs (as group). Two armchairs and four side chairs; the cantilevered seat with spindled back and curved crest rail; armchairs 39 inches high; side chairs 36 inches high; $2,760.

Miscellaneous

George Nakashima Chest of Drawers. Vertical; rectangular top with dovetailed edges with six drawers and a very thin drawer at the top; on sled base; 53 inches high × 20 inches deep × 36¼ inches wide; $1,725.

George Nakashima Walnut Buffet. Sliding spindle doors with brass cloth backing; one side opens to reveal an interior fitted with adjustable shelves, the other side reveals fitted drawers; top has dovetailed edge on one side and free-form slab on the other; on geometric base; 32½ inches high × 29½ inches deep × 75¼ inches wide; $1,840.

George Nakashima Walnut Credenza. Sliding spindle doors with brass cloth backing open to reveal interior fitted with adjustable shelves; topped with a thin compartmented drawer, top has two hinged leaves with free edges; on geometric base; 32 inches high × 18⅛ inches deep × 60¾ inches wide; $2,530.

Burled Wood Screen, in the manner of George Nakashima, c. 1965. Thick irregular slab mounted on a gnarled burled wood base; unsigned; 60 inches high × 50 inches wide; unusual; $920.

GEORGE NELSON (1908–1986)

Nelson, best known for his furniture designs, studied to be an architect at Yale University. He also became a writer and teacher. While acting as co-managing editor of *Architectural Forum* from 1943 to 1944, he was influenced by the work of the International Style architects. In 1946 he became design director of the Herman Miller Furniture Company, where he remained until his death in 1986. Many of his designs, along with those of designers who worked on his staff, are still considered unique. Among them the Coconut chair (1956), the Sling sofa (1964), and the first pole system in America, Omni (1956), created for Aluminum Extrusions. In 1947 he opened his own design studio, even while continuing to work for Herman Miller. He authored many important books on design over the years.

In the 60s and 70s he was a pioneer in designing office furniture systems for Herman Miller that tied in with the new attitudes and designs of those decades. They are collectible in their own right.

PRICES

George Nelson Action Office System Desk, manufactured by Herman Miller, c. 1964. Sculptural four-drawer unit with roll top of alternating walnut and ash slats; desk top of pale gray laminate; filing bin of molded plywood laminate; asymmetrical side panels of black molded plastic; legs of cast aluminum, chrome-plated foot rail; 44 inches long × 34 inches deep × 64 inches wide; excellent condition; roll top recabled; $750.

ISAMU NOGUCHI (1904–1988)

Noguchi is considered one of the most important American sculptors of the twentieth century; he contributed many designs for furniture and decorative arts that are equally noteworthy. He was influenced by his Japanese father and his American mother, and also by a two-country education. In the late 40s he made a series of sculptures in the new biomorphic forms. His first furniture designs were also biomorphic (1939). In 1944 he worked on biomorphic furniture for the Herman Miller Furniture Company. In the following years he created his Akari lamps (1951), a version of traditional Japanese lanterns. He designed various versions of the Akari lamps for the next twenty-five years. In 1985 the Isamu Noguchi Garden Museum in Long Island City opened, displaying his sculptural gardens in rough, primal stone—obviously inspired by Japanese gardens.

PRICES

Isamu Noguchi Cocktail Table, manufactured by Herman Miller, c. 1970s. Two-part adjustable base in natural walnut finish; round triangular glass top; 16 inches high × 36 inches deep × 50 inches wide; excellent condition; $1,100.

EERO SAARINEN (1910–1961)

Saarinen came by his talent naturally. His father, Finnish architect Eliel Saarinen, helped establish and became president of

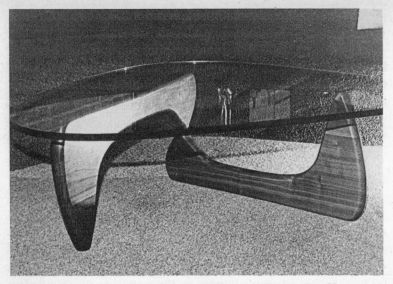

Cocktail table, designed by Isamu Noguchi, manufactured by Herman Miller, c. 1970s. Two-part, adjustable base in natural walnut finish, round triangular glass top; 16 inches high × 36 inches deep × 50 inches wide; $246. Courtesy of Toomey-Treadway Galleries, Oak Park, IL.

the Cranbrook Academy of Art in Bloomfield Hills, Michigan. His mother was a respected textile designer.

The family came to the United States in 1923. Eero worked on designing furniture from 1929 to 1933 for the neighboring Kingwood School for Girls—the building itself was designed by his father. From 1939 to 1942 Eero acted as assistant in the Department of Architecture at Cranbrook. He collaborated with Charles Eames and won two prizes—for introducing the three-dimensionally molded shell and for modular furniture. In 1943 Saarinen began designing furniture for Knoll Associates. His first chair of 1943 was of bent plywood. In 1946 he designed the first fiberglass chair to be mass produced in the United States, the #70 lounge chair. The most important of his designs utilized his architectural and furniture knowledge and combined them with new materials. These "pedestal" pieces, designed for Knoll (1955–1957), used the molded shell concept for chairs. The chairs were aluminum with a fused plastic finish with fiberglass and nylon upholstery.

There were many copies of the pedestal armchair made during the 50s and 60s. Collectors should study the beauty of his original proportions—not found in the copies. The side chairs and tables in the pedestal line are still being produced by Knoll.

PRICES

Womb Chair, designed by Eero Saarinen, c. 1965. Orange plastic; $2,400.

Eero Saarinen Side Table, manufactured by Knoll. Elegant pedestal form of white enameled aluminum base; beveled walnut top; 21 inches high × 20 inches in diameter; excellent condition; $210.

Upholstered Dining Chairs (eight), design attributed to Eero Saarinen, manufactured by Knoll Associates, c. 1960. Molded bow-shaped back with demilune cut at base; back and seat upholstered in red vinyl; raised on four stainless steel tubular legs; manufacturer's label; 36 inches high; $300/set.

CHARLES STENDIG

Although this firm manufactured furniture in the 1950s, it became important in the 1960s and 1970s for its use of plastics and Pop elements in furniture design. Among the most notable pieces are the Gyro chair, designed by Eero Aarnio, and the Marilyn sofa. The original Marilyn love seat was inspired by Mae West's face. (In 1937 Salvador Dali designed a room meant to represent West's face, with her red lips forming a sofa. Unlike the later plastic Marilyn sofa, it was upholstered.) Both the Gyro chair and the Marilyn sofa are still being made.

PRICES

DePas D'Urbino Lomazzi "Joe" Chair, manufactured by Stendig, c. 1960s. Two-seat baseball glove sofa; molded foam over spring steel frame on coasters; original black leather upholstery; 40 inches high × 62 inches long × 32 inches deep; excellent condition; $8,500.

Marilyn Lips Sofa, after Salvador Dali design (c. 1934), c. 1975. Red nylon upholstery over foam rubber and plastic frame; unsigned; 33½ inches high × 31 inches deep × 82 inches long; stains; $2,310.

Eero Aarnio Gyro Chair, c. 1967. Finland winner of the A.I.D. award in 1968; vibrant orange cut-out bulbous form of molded glass-reinforced polyester; has been shown as everything from indoor rocker to outdoor pool or sleigh; marked "MADE IN FINLAND"; 22 inches high × 34 inches deep × 34 inches wide; excellent condition; $750.

Gyro Chairs (pair), designed by Eero Aarnio, c. 1960s. Each white; lacquered and molded plastic; $489/set.

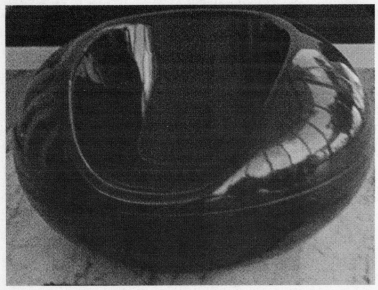

Gyro Chair, designed by Eero Aarnio, c. 1968. Fiberglass, red; $1,500. Courtesy of Al Eiber Collection.

Cabinet, designed by Paul Evans, manufactured by Directional, c. 1970. Innovative use of color and texture using welded sheets of steel and enamel to create an abstract decoration in relief, top of inset slate, floating on recessed platform; 27 inches high × 23 inches deep × 96 inches wide; $900. Courtesy of Toomey-Treadway Galleries, Oak Park, IL.

❋ OTHER AMERICAN FURNITURE DESIGNS ❋

PRICES

Cocktail Table, c. 1960s. Round glass top on aluminum bent propeller-shaped base; 14 inches high × 42 inches in diameter; excellent condition; $425.

Maple Side Table, designed by Tom Barry (a student of Wendell Castle). Rectangular top on zigzag cut legs; $200.

❋ ITALIAN FURNITURE ❋

Several distinctive furniture designs came out of Italy following World War II. One of them was adjustable furniture using the new Modern concepts and materials. One of the important designers was Osvaldo Borsani, who was previously recognized

Pedestal Table, designed by Richard Schetz, 1960s. Cast aluminum;
$250. Courtesy of Skank World.

Andirons, designed by Donald Deskey, manufactured by Bennett Ireland,
Inc., c. 1960. Brass Finished tapering blade on cast-iron base, marked
BENNETT; *19¼ inches high, overall depth 18¾ inches; $275.* Courtesy of
Skinner Inc., Boston Bolton, MA.

for his Traditional furniture. The new adjustable pieces were manufactured beginning in 1954 by Techno S.p.A., the firm owned by the Borsani family. His first adjustable design was a divan bed called D70, made with metal frames and polyfoam upholstery. It was unique because it was multifunctional, changing from a seat to a bed or a storage piece. His next piece, the P40 lounge chair, offered even more complicated mechanical variety, and in design showed organic curves that softened the look. For the ultimate in comfort it shifted to three positions.

Marco Zanusco, working around the same time, created his Lady chair in 1951. This chair originated a new form of upholstered furniture using rubber webbing as the support and foam rubber for padding. Another of his "firsts" was the Sleep-O-Matic sofa bed. It was constructed in 1954 with the same tubular steel frame and upholstery as his earlier easy chair. These and other later pieces were manufactured by Arflex.

Another significant contributor to postwar furniture designs was Carlo Mollino, whose experiments with form led to such classics as his biomorphic table Arabesco. Trained as an architect, he originally designed furniture for his clients. The Arabesco was such a piece, and was treated as sculpture.

While new forms verging on fantasy were part of the furniture designed in the 70s, both in Europe and the United States, some of the most unusual examples came out of Italy. They took new plastics and turned them into sculptural furniture designs from the simple to the elaborate. ABS plastic, both strong, and nonreinforced, was used for injection-molded pieces.

By the 60s many small Italian factories were using American industrial methods to turn out furnishings made of the new plastic materials. Among them were Arflex (Studio Zanuso), Artemide, Cassina, and Gufram.

MARIO BELLINI (1935–)

This architect and designer studied architecture at the Politecnico in Milan, then went on to establish the Studio Bellini Architecture and Industrial Design Office in the same city in 1973. From there he designed for such firms as Artemide, B & B Italia, Olivetti, Yamaha, and others. His works are in collections at the Museum of Modern Art in New York, Studie Archivo della Communicazione, and Musee des Arts Decoratifs in Montreal.

Among his noteworthy designs are the Programma 101 microcomputer terminal for Olivetti, 1965; Amanta and Bamole chairs and Quattro Gatti tables for B & B Italia, 1966–1972; Totem radio and record player in lacquered wood housing for Brionvega, 1971; Area 50 table lamps in porcelain and plastic

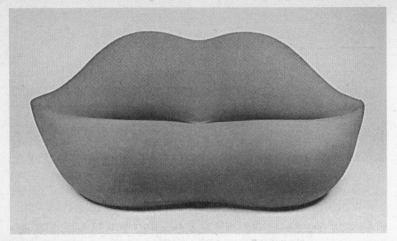

Love Seat, "The Marilyn," designed by Studio 65 for Gufram in the 1960s. In the form of lips, formed of molded foam, usually covered in lipstick-red nylon, Italy; $1,500. Courtesy of Toomey-Treadway Galleries, Oak Park, IL.

for Artemide, 1975; and Cab chair in steel and leather for Cassina, 1977.

ANNA CASTELLI-FERRIERI (1920–   )

This architect and industrial designer studied at the University of Milan (1938–1943) and began work as a free-lance architect in 1946. Among the firms she has designed for are Kartell, Nirvana, Oltolini, and Apelli e Varesio. She was a founding member of Movimento Studi per l'Architettura in Milan. Her work is in the collections of the Museum of Modern Art, New York; Israel Museum, Jerusalem; Design Museum, London; and others. Among her best-known designs are modular system kitchen furniture for Oltolini, 1950; square stacking units in ABS plastic for Kartell, 1967; oval table in fiberglass for Kartell, 1969; and multiuse stools in polypropylene and metal for Kartell, 1977.

CESARE (JOE) COLOMBO (1930–1971)

A versatile designer, Italian-born Colombo trained as an architect. In 1962 he began working as an industrial designer. How-

Wall Unit, designed by Joe Colombo, manufactured by Intrruttore, c. 1969. Lighted wall unit, sold by the piece, made of white polyester reinforced plastic; $1,300. Courtesy of Anthony Du Pont Collection.

ever, he is best known today for his furniture. His use of materials and techniques merged with his skill as a sculptor in his 1965 design for stacking side chairs. They were made of injection-molded ABS plastic by the Kartell Company—among the first Italian manufacturers to use plastics in household items.

Collectors should look for the following identifying marks impressed on the underside of the seat: sometimes "KARTELL, BINASCO (Milano) 860 e 861 1 5 [within a circle] MADE IN ITALY/ DESIGN Prof. Joe Colombo (model no. 4860)"; other times "model 4860, KARTELL[(R)]/designer: JOE COLOMBO/made in U.S.A. by/Beylerian L.T.D."

KARTELL S.p.A.

Kartell was one of the first companies in Italy to produce plastic items. The company, founded by Giulio Castelli in 1949, used

Tube Chair, designed by Joe Colombo, manufactured by Flexform, c. 1970. Plastic, polyurethane and synthetic knot upholstery; largest tube measures 25¼ inches high × 19⅜ inches wide; $1,500. Courtesy of Anthony Du Pont Collection.

bright colors for small housewares designed by Gino Columbini. By the 1960s the company used name Italian designers to create its expanded line, which included furniture and decorative pieces. Among the top names who designed for Kartell was Joe Colombo, who created a full-size dining chair molded in one piece.

GAETANO PESCE (1939–)

This innovative architectural, graphic, and interior designer studied architecture at the University of Venice (1959–1965). Later, as a free-lance designer, his commissions included jobs for Knoll, Venini, and Cassina. His furniture designs incorporated the new plastics and mixed materials. One of his more famous furniture designs was the UP 1 chair of 1969. He created

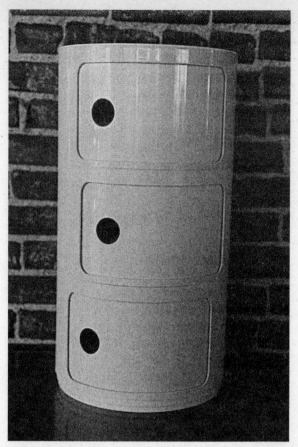

Stackable Units, designed by Anna Castelli-Ferrieri, c. 1960s. White, ABC plastic; each approximately 36 inches high; set of six; $250. Courtesy of Skank World.

a polyurethane foam shape and covered it with stretch nylon and wool jersey. It was unique in that it came compressed in a package that expanded to the correct shape and size when opened. It is typical of the 1960s Italian design concepts that took advantage of newly developed materials to produce a different structural form.

Some of Pesce's important designs include:

Table, designed by Giotto Stoppino, manufactured by Kartell, c. 1967. Black, molded plastic, 18 × 18 inches; $150. Courtesy of Fat Chance.

- UP self-inflating chairs in polyurethane foam and synthetic jersey for C & B Italia, 1969.
- Sit-down upholstered seating group in polyurethane foam and Dacron, made for Cassina, 1975.

PRICES

Chair, Birch; female form; $4,000.

GIOVANNI (GIO) PONTI (1891–1979)
This versatile architect and designer is considered one of Italy's most important creative influences. He led Italy back to the

---

forefront in post–World War II design with his furniture and glasswork. His decorative objects and furniture can be recognized by their sleek, tapering, and curving forms. In the 1940s and 1950s he created vividly colored glassware for Venini. Among his interior designs for Italian ships were those he executed for the S.S. *Andrea Doria.* In the field of furniture, he created pieces for Knoll, Arflex, Cassina, and Techno in the 1950s and 1960s. They are noted for their simplistic elegance. His Superleggera (meaning extralight) side chair, model 699, is an example of his use of Traditional design translated into Modern Form. It combined ash, rush, and steel glides.

PRICES

Cantilevered Desk, design attributed to Giovanni Ponti, manufactured by Brutten, c. 1962. Also known as the Buck

Side Chair, designed by Gio Ponti, c. 1960. Aluminum with black plastic seat; 31 inches high; $150. Courtesy of Skank World.

Rogers Desk; weighted cylindrical pedestal with two drawers; stainless steel banding at top and bottom; long lacquered writing surface; 30 inches high × 30 inches deep × 84 inches wide; very good condition; recent black lacquer; $400.

❀ OTHER ITALIAN FURNITURE DESIGNS ❀

PRICES

Toga Chair, designed by Sergio Mazza, manufactured by Artimede. Vibrant orange sculptural form of molded fiberglass-reinforced polyester; 24 inches high × 28 inches deep × 28 inches wide; excellent condition; $350.

Cleopatra Sofa, designed by Geoffrey Harcourt/Artifort, c. 1973. Orange stretch jersey–covered foam; tubular steel frame supported on metal casters; unusual sculptural form; 26 inches high × 34 inches deep × 74 inches long; very good condition; tiny puncture on lower bottom; $2,000.

Eco and Luisa Peresi Ash-Veneered Plywood and Painted Steel Table, manufactured for Atamira, c. 1960. Circular top inlaid with a swirling pattern of ash veneers; raised on a pedestal base with three angled legs painted black; retains original retailer's label; 27½ inches high × 33⅝ inches in diameter; $1,840.

❀ FRENCH FURNITURE ❀

OLIVIER MOURGUE (1939–)
One of the important industrial designers during the 1960s and 1970s, Mourgue began his education at the Lycée Pasteur in Paris, attending from 1946 to 1954. He studied interior design at the Ecole Boulle, also in Paris, from 1954 to 1960. He received degrees from the Architectural Institute and the Ecole Nationale Supérieure des Arts Decoratifs. From 1959 he was a freelance designer, finally opening a studio in 1966.

His most famous furniture design, the Djinn chair, made in

1964–1965, was used in the film *2001: A Space Odyssey* and reflected what Mourgue felt would be the furniture of the future.

Other collectible Mourgue designs include:

- Montreal shell-structure armchair in polyester with loose cushions, designed for Airborne, 1966.

- Fleur lamp series of chromed metal and aluminum, designed for Editions Pierre Disderot, 1967.

- Cubic armchair with polyester shell and loose jersey cushion, designed for Airborne, 1968.

PRICES

Olivier Mourgue Bench, manufactured by Airborne International, France. Backless two-seat version of sofa constructed of molded steel frame; upholstered in polyurethane foam covered in black nylon stretch fabric; 14 inches high × 22 inches deep × 48 inches wide; very good condition; $1,700.

Olivier Mourgue Settee, manufactured by Airborne International, France. Sculptural form of molded steel frame; upholstered in polyurethane foam covered in black nylon stretch fabric; produced from 1965 to 1976; seen in the 1968 film *2001: A Space Odyssey*; 29 inches high × 29 inches deep × 46 inches wide; very good condition; minor run in nylon; $2,200.

Olivier Mourgue Lounge Chair and Ottoman, manufactured by Airborne International, France. Sculptural form of molded steel; upholstered in polyurethane foam covered in black nylon stretch fabric; chair 26 inches high × 24 inches deep × 24 inches wide; ottoman 14 inches high × 23 inches deep × 26 inches wide; very good condition; overall normal wear; $950.

Olivier Mourgue Lounge Chair and Ottoman, manufactured

Furniture Grouping, designed by Olivier Mourgue, manufactured by Airborne International France. Consisting of 4 pieces; $850. Courtesy of Treadway Gallery.

by Airborne International, France. Sculptural form of molded steel; upholstered in polyurethane foam covered in black nylon stretch fabric; chair 26 inches high × 24 inches deep × 24 inches wide; ottoman 14 inches high × 23 inches deep × 26 inches wide; very good condition; $850.

Olivier Mourgue Djinn Chaise Longue, c. 1963. Avant-garde sculptural form of molded steel frame and reupholstered foam in black wool; 25 inches high × 23 inches deep × 63 inches long; very good condition; $800.

Pierre Paulin

Pierre Paulin created designs for Artifort. He is well known for his metal-and-chrome chairs dating from 1963 to 1965.

PRICES

Armchairs (pair), design attributed to Pierre Paulin, c. 1960. Sculptural forms with seat and back separated by curved

---

"The Easy Chair 577," designed by Pierre Paulin manufacturers, by Artifort Company, 1967. Red, polyurethane and synthetic knit upholstery; $2,300. Courtesy of Anthony Du Pont Collection.

chrome support; swivel base; beige wool upholstery; 31 inches high × 24 inches deep × 28 inches wide; excellent condition; $300.

Fauteuil 562 Black Jersey Chair and Ottoman, designed by Pierre Paulin for Artifort, c. 1960. Circular seat with waisted sides; convered with black jersey; with matching pouf; 25 inches high × 19 inches deep × 34¼ inches wide; ottoman 19¼ inches in diameter; $2,860/set.

The Easy Chair 577, designed by Pierre Paulin, manufactured by Artifort Company, 1967. Red polyurethane and synthetic knit upholstery; $2,300.

JEAN PROUVÉ (1901–1984)

Trained as an architect, he also became a skilled iron craftsman. These two skills were combined in his furniture designs, beginning in 1924. He was among the first French designers to consider mass production a viable way to create furniture. While his pre–World War II designs seem industrial in appearance, by the 1950s his furniture had become more appealing to consumers. How he felt about his designs can be summed up in his own words: "There is no difference between the building of furniture and the building of a house." His furniture combined U-beams, steel tubing, and laminated woods.

Other notable French designers of the period include:

- Charlotte Perriand
  Architect
- Serge Mouille
  Silversmith. His lighting designs were of aluminum in mobile style forms.
- Jean Royere
  Worked in woods and metals, creating furniture

❀ SCANDINAVIAN FURNITURE ❀

EERO AARNIO (1932–   )

Probably Finland's most important architect and designer, Eero Aarnio brought Finnish designs to world prominence in the 1960s. He was educated at the School of Industrial Design in Helsinki from 1954 to 1957. His early designs were influenced by Finnish traditions and materials. However, he began innovating with new forms and plastics in the 1960s. He is famed for his Ball and Bubble chairs, strictly avant-garde pieces based on traditionally oriented Finnish designs. In 1962 he opened his own design studio, creating furniture and interior designs.

TAPIO WIRKKALA (1915–1985)

Famed Finnish industrial designer and sculptor Tapio Wirkkala created influential works until 1984. His career began in the postwar era when Scandinavian design was dominant. He studied sculpture at the School of Industrial Arts, Helsinki, Finland. From 1946 to 1985 he was a glass designer for Karhula-litala.

Ball Chair, designed by Eero Aarnio, manufactured by Asko Finnternational, Helsinki, Finland, c. 1963–1965. Space-age influence, fiberglass, aluminum, synthetic foam and wool upholstery; 47 inches high × 40¾ inches deep × 37½ inches wide. Courtesy of Modern Props.

Hanging Globe Chair, designed by Eero Aarnio, c. 1953–1965. Also pictured, floor lamp, brass with adjustable painted metal shade, cone-shaped, c. 1953, exhibited at the Milan Triennale; $2,500. Courtesy of Al Eiber Collection.

He was also the founder and director of Tapio Wirkkala Design Studio, in Helsinki, from 1955. His work in glass and laminated wood serving pieces won many awards over the years. He was hired as an industrial designer to create products in ceramics, silver, glass, and wood.

PRICES

Inlaid Teak and Chromed Metal Coffee Table, c. 1960. Rectangular top inlaid with oval devices in light and dark wood raised on four tapering chromed metal legs ending in brass feet; branded "TAPIO WIRKKALA/ASKO/MADE IN FINLAND"; 15¾ inches high × 48¾ inches long × 24⅜ inches wide; $2,012.

VERNER PANTON (1926–)

An architect and industrial designer of many talents, Panton is recognized primarily for his chair designs, which featured a variety of materials. However, his creative designs include textiles, lighting, and other products. This Danish architect's Cone chair of 1958 brought him early recognition in contemporary design. After studying at the Royal Danish Academy of Fine Arts, Copenhagen, from 1947 to 1951, he became an associate with Arne Jacobsen (1950–1952) and went on to form his own architectural and design office in Denmark (1955–1962). In 1963 he moved his work to Binningen, Switzerland. He is known for making the first single-piece plastic chair. The design dates from 1960, but because of technical production problems, it wasn't until 1968 that it was produced—by Vitra GmbH

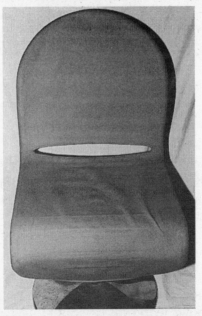

Tongue Chair, designed by Vernor Panton. Sculptural steel upholstered in stretch canvas, highly polished chrome disc base; 34 inches high × 22 inches deep × 19 inches wide; $300. Courtesy Toomey-Treadway Galleries, Oak Park, IL.

(Basel, Switzerland) for Herman Miller International, New York. This side chair was in production from 1968 to 1979. It became popular as one of the Pop designs of the 1960s.

PRICES

Verner Panton Cone Chair, c. 1959. Bent chromium steel cage construction; pony skin seat; 30 inches high × 24 inches deep × 24 inches wide; excellent condition; $1,700.

Verner Panton Cone Chair, c. 1959. Bright orange upholstery, bent sheet metal construction; 32 inches high × 24 inches deep × 23 inches wide; excellent condition; $1,100.

Stacking Chair, designed by Verner Panton, manufactured by Herman Miller Company, 1960. Orange plastic; $300.

❈ OTHER INTERNATIONAL FURNITURE DESIGNS ❈

JAN EKSELIUS

PRICES

Jan Sofa and Ottoman, designed by Jan Ekselius, c. 1970. Sable stretch velour fabric covering polyurethane foam molded directly onto a bent and welded steel spring frame; very sculptural form; chair 31 inches high × 43 inches deep × 24 inches wide; ottoman 14 inches high × 24 inches deep × 19 inches wide; excellent condition; $240.

ROBERTO SEBASTIAN MATTA (1911–)

Though well known in the 40s as a Surrealist painter, this controversial Chilean artist turned his hand to designing quintessential Pop Art furniture in the 60s and 70s. One of his best known pieces was a set of seating furniture in puzzle form,

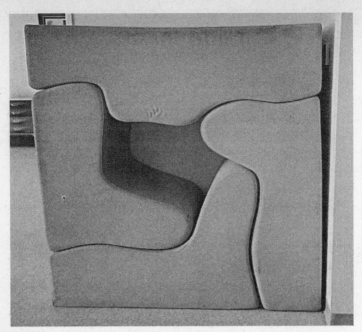

Seating System, "The Malitte," designed by Roberto Sebastian Matta,
produced by Gavina, Italy, for Knoll Associates, c. 1966. Elastic wool
with polyurethane foam and stretch wool upholstery; $4,300. Courtesy of
Anthony Du Pont Collection.

Malitte, done for the Italian furniture maker Dino Gavina. According to legend, Matta was given a large block of polyurethane foam. He designed four seats cut from the edge of the
block and then rounded the remaining center section, which
was to be an ottoman. Each piece was upholstered, with seats
in one color and the ottoman in another.

Glass

One of the fastest growing collectible fields is 60s, 70s glass. This includes not only commercial pieces from the United States, Europe, and Scandinavia, but the more expensive studio glass pieces. Recently Italian glass from the 30s, 40s and 50s commanded all the attention at auctions, but now Scandinavian glass is inching up in price. Dan Ripley, a second generation 20th century glass dealer, recently pointed out that it is the collectors who are doing the buying at auctions specializing in glass from mid-century and beyond. "You have to know the difference between artistic and commercial glass," he said. "As far as Italian glass is concerned, the end of the 60s is pretty much the final phase of the quality Italian glass makers are noted for. Collectors are looking to the more interesting Scandinavian designers like Ulrica Vallien and her husband, Bertil Vallien, and others of the Kosta Boda group."

Steuben glass from the 60s and 70s, mentioned here in detail, is beginning to turn up at auctions priced at a fraction of its original retail price. Even the limited edition pieces by such noted glass designers as Donald Pollard and Lloyd Atkins, are current auction bargains.

The most exciting possibilities from both a collecting and an investment point of view, are American Studio glass. While it is relatively expensive at the quality Crafts shows, it can be quite affordable at auction. Names to watch out for are listed in the following pages.

❀ UNITED STATES ❀

STEUBEN

The Steuben glassworks was founded in 1903 by Frederick Carder. It was a time of new ideas and the growth of art glass on both sides of the Atlantic. Carder came to Corning, New York, from England at the same time Louis Comfort Tiffany was developing his new concepts in American art glass. Color was all-important to the glass developed at Steuben, along with the use of new techniques. During the thirty years Steuben was under the direction of Carder, hundred of different colors and thousands of forms were produced. By the end of World War II, a new trend began at Orrefors and Kosta glassworks in Sweden. It explored the optical properties of glass and the newly popular geometric and other forms.

When Arthur A. Houghton, Jr., became president of Steuben in 1933, he banished color. With a team of architects and artists, the Scandinavian techniques were combined with a newly developed optical glass composition that offered an unusual brilliance. In 1935, in keeping with the new approach, a series of decorative pieces were made by Sidney Waugh using copper wheel and diamond-point engraving, a process which produced a look similar to the Swedish style.

In 1937 architect John Gates met with Henri Matisse in Paris. As a result Matisse volunteered to make a drawing to be engraved on a Steuben piece. A great idea was born. Gates commissioned drawings from other important European and American painters and sculptors for a line that became "Design in Glass by Twenty-seven Contemporary Artists."

Like many American companies, from furniture to silver manufacturers, Steuben's output was changed by United States participation in World War II. Not until the 50s did Steuben regain its place as an innovator of quality, with such important designers as Sidney Waugh, Donald Pollard, Don Wier, George Thompson, and Lloyd Atkins leading the way.

After World War II Steuben produced full-lead crystal, and Arthur Houghton commissioned internationally famed artists to design for Steuben. In the year from 1954 to 1955 artists from the Near and Far East created a series of designs for Steuben that were later displayed at the National Gallery of Art in Washington in its "Asian Artists in Crystal" exhibition.

During the 50s major ornamental pieces were produced. And in 1959, a group of thirty-one "collector's pieces" in engraved crystal showcased Steuben's own designers. In a sense, this glass from the 50s began a new form of American art glass. The pieces were always high priced, and available only in limited number. When they come to market, and that's rarely, they still go for top dollar.

More affordable are the tableware, barware, and nonengraved decorative pieces. They rely on their form for appeal, often the free forms or undulating curves of the Modern design era. Many of these pieces were designed by Donald Pollard, who also created important limited-edition engraved pieces.

From the mid-50s to the 70s free sculptural forms of crystal and animal and bird figures were produced.

By the 60s designers such as Donald Pollard, Paul Schulze, Lloyd Atkins, Eric Hilton, and George Thompson turned their talents to the shapes and look of Postmodern designs. Convolution II, designed in 1969 by Paul Schulze, is a good example.

During the 1970s crystal was often sandblasted or combined with precious metal to achieve the tortured look found in 70s sculpture. These one-of-a-kind pieces cost thousands of dollars at the time of production and rarely come to market.

Mass-produced vases often used the air-bubble-in-the-base technique pioneered in the 1950s by Timo Sarpaneva. When they come to auction, prices are modest, compared to their original cost.

Though they are not examples of Postmodern design, Steuben's small sculptures of birds, fish, and animals from the 1970s can form an inexpensive collection.

PRICES

Crystal Sculpture of Cupola with Golden Whale. Signed on crystal cupola with vermeil whale weather vane above; with red leather case; 7¾ inches high; $700.

Crystal Long Bowl, designed by George Thompson, c. 1964. Numbered "SP993"; signed "STEUBEN"; 22 inches wide; $450.

LLOYD ATKINS
This Brooklyn-born designer began his studies in design at Brooklyn's Pratt Institute in 1941. The following year he joined

the United States Air Force. When World War II ended, he returned to Pratt and graduated with a Certificate of Industrial Design. He joined the Steuben Glass design department in 1948, and by continuing his studies at night, he earned his B.I.D. degree from Pratt. His designs in crystal have been included in many Steuben exhibits both here and abroad.

PRICES

Crystal Duckling, designed by Lloyd Atkins, c. 1964. Numbered "8129"; signed "STEUBEN"; $350.

Crystal Lyre Vase, designed by Lloyd Atkins, c. 1962. Numbered "8113"; signed "STEUBEN"; $300.

Crystal Frog, designed by Lloyd Atkins, c. 1961. Numbered "8109"; signed "STEUBEN"; $300.

JAMES HOUSTON

In 1962 this artist, naturalist, and writer joined the design department of Steuben Glass, where his interest in nature was reflected in his glass sculptures. His education includes the study of painting and graphic arts in his native Canada, Paris, and Tokyo. Subsequently he spent twelve years as a civil administrator for the Canadian government in the eastern Arctic, where he helped promote worldwide exhibits of Eskimo art. He has written and illustrated several books, including a novel titled *The White Dawn*. While at Steuben he was among the artists who began combining glass with rich metals in his designs. "I am interested in having the glass say something to you. You look and you respond because you know *what it is*. My glass has to tell a story. I am not interested in abstract forms and I could never do them."

Recently some of Houston's works have come to auction, among them "Thistle Rock" and "Excalibur," originally made in 1977. They sell for relatively modest prices, compared with the 1977 retail prices, and represent a "sleeper" for collectors.

Glass Sculptures. Left: *Excalibur, designed by James Houston for Steuben, c. 1977, $1,900; center: Thistle Rock, designed by James Houston, c. 1977, signed, $1,800; right: Trout and Fly, designed by James Houston, c. 1966, signed, $1,500.*

PRICES

Crystal-and-Gold Trout and Fly Sculpture, designed by James Houston, c. 1966. Fish leaping; hooked by 18K gold Royal Coachman; signed in script "STEUBEN"; with original red-velvet-lined conforming box; 9½ inches high; $1,500.

Crystal Sculpture of Excalibur. Crystal rock; inset with sterling sword; signed; with red leather case 8½ inches high; $1,900.

Crystal Sculpture of Thistle Rock. Crystal rock with vermeil thistle above; signed; with red leather case; 7½ inches high; $1,800.

DONALD POLLARD

This painter and designer became a staff designer for Steuben Glass in 1950. He is a graduate of the Rhode Island School of Design. He was also in the trainee program of the Institute of

Contemporary Art in Boston, where he worked in silver. In addition he worked in architectural theater design. He was the first Steuben designer to combine glass with precious metals in the 1960s. His work is represented in public and private collections around the world and in such museums as the Metropolitan Museum of Art in New York and the National Gallery of Modern Art in New Delhi, India.

PRICES

Crystal Cat, designed by Donald Pollard, c. 1960. Number "8102"; signed "STEUBEN"; $350.

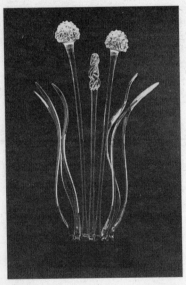 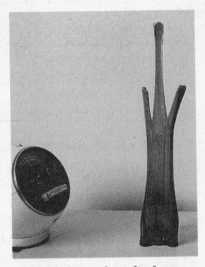

Crystal Arrangement, c. 1979. Ten individual glass rods as freeform blossoms, seed pods, stems, inserted into rectangular glass box/vase with openings for additional components, impressed CARTIER, *artist signed; total height: 23 inches; $600.* Courtesy of Skinner Inc., Boston/Bolton, MA.

Glass Vase, c. 1960s. American, orange; 26 inches high; $75. Courtesy of Anthony Du Pont Collection.

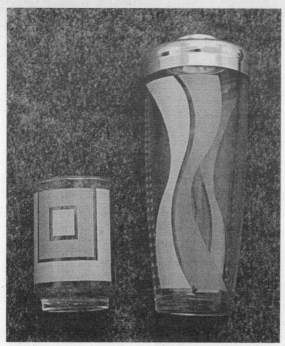

Cocktail Set, early 1970s. American, glass, shaker and four glasses, Irvin Ware manufacturers; $45. Courtesy of Anthony Du Pont Collection.

❋ AMERICAN STUDIO GLASS ❋

Since the 1960s the whole concept of glassmaking has changed. Through the efforts and experiments of glass artists and technicians such as pioneers Harvey Littleton, Dominick Labino, Dale Chihuly, and Marvin Lipofsky, blown glass and glass in general have become media for the artist—an art not a craft.

During those early years, Americans bought whatever caught the eye, mostly at craft fairs, street fairs, and craft galleries. Only a few buyers thought of themselves as serious collectors. They were attracted to a piece because it fit in with their antiestablishment decor or represented an exciting new collecting category. Much of the work done then was in hot glass.

The work from the 1960s was largely experimental. Since it was a new creative area there was no one to criticize it.

Another reason for working with and collecting studio glass of the 60s was because of what it represented—the individual craftsman working against organized society and mass-produced wares of all kinds. It was part of the craft revival era, when "doing your own thing" was more important than making money.

By 1971 there were two galleries offering the new glass. They were Heller Gallery in New York and Habatat in Michigan. Today not only are there several thousand glass artists working but corresponding galleries from coast to coast offering their works.

What began with classes and programs at the University of Wisconsin, taught by Harvey Littleton, has now expanded to glass courses in universities and workshops across the country. In addition, many artists continue to set up workshops on their own.

It was in the 1960s that artists realized what they could do with glass was almost limitless. They created sculpture, making shapes in hot glass. What was experimental in the early 1960s became established working methods, and by the 1970s they had experimented with other techniques such as slumping and casting using cold processes. All allowed them to widen the range of possible forms. Artists also incorporated other materials into their glass designs.

The legacy of Harvey Littleton continues with new generations of glassblowing artists. Foremost is Dale Chihuly. Others whose work sells for thousands of dollars are Dan Dailey and Marvin Lipofsky, who, like Chihuly, studied with Littleton.

DALE CHIHULY (1941–   )

An early leader of the contemporary studio glass movement, he has drawn blown glass into the category of fine art. In the mid-70s there was little demand for contemporary art glass in

America, but today collectors spend in the high thousands for his work.

He graduated from the University of Washington, where he experimented with weaving glass, and from there went on to an architectural firm as an interior designer. In 1966 he enrolled in Harvey Littleton's postgraduate glass class. (Littleton, who founded the studio glass movement in 1962, is mentioned elsewhere in this book.) After more degrees and study he got a Fulbright Fellowship to Italy, where he was able to apprentice at the Venini glass factory. By 1971, with the aid of John Hauberg, Hauberg's wife, Anne Gould Hauberg, and a $2,000 grant from the Union of Independent Colleges of Art, he founded an art glass colony. It was called Pilchuck, after its location in Pilchuck Creek in Washington State. The school has grown and is steadily turning out new generations of promising glassblowers and artists.

Today the Chihuly studio, known as "the boathouse," is on Lake Union, north of downtown Seattle. It has glory holes, or glass furnaces, thirty-six inches high on the interior, designed with a series of doors that can be adjusted to accommodate the pieces being blown. When a glory hole is opened all the way, two million BTUs of heat—2,500 degrees Fahrenheit—surge forward as the glass is being shaped. As Chihuly puts it, "You're working with fire, which is really the tool."

Chihuly himself hasn't blown glass since a 1976 auto accident injured an eye. His work today is the result of drawing, designing, and directing his skilled team.

His inspirations can come with chance encounters with colors or forms. A perfect example of the result of such an encounter is his Pilchuck Basket series of 1977. While visiting the Tacoma Historical Society, a pile of Northwest Coast Indian baskets that were stacked one inside another caught his eye. "They were dented and misshapen, wonderful forms," he has said. "I don't really know what made me want to reproduce them in glass, but that was my mission for the summer." Other influences have been forms and colors of the sea and the glass of Venice.

His work is represented in many permanent collections. It can be seen in the Rainbow Room Complex at Rockefeller Center in New York, where the large blown-glass forms appear to float off the wall, dramatized by lighting. It is also a part of the collections of the Los Angeles County Museum of Art; the Metropolitan Museum of Art, New York; the Museum of Fine Arts, Boston; the Smithsonian Institution, Washington, D.C.; the National Museum of Modern Art, Kyoto, Japan; and the Victoria and Albert Museum, London.

PRICES

Blanket Cylinder, designed by Dale Chihuly, 1975. Blown glass; signed with initials, shamrock, and dated "75" in glass threads; 9¼ inches high; $8,000.

Three Baskets, designed by Dale Chihuly, 1979. Blown glass; trailed decoration; signed and dated "79"; heights: 5 inches × 6 inches in diameter, 5½ inches × 5¼ inches in diameter, 3½ inches × 4 inches in diameter; $2,000.

MICHAEL HIGGINS (1908–   )
FRANCES HIGGINS (1912–   )

A lifelong shared career as glass artists began for Michael and Frances Higgins over forty years ago, when both were university teachers. For Frances, it began as a hobby in 1942, when she became interested in working with sheet glass. When she and Michael (who was British by birth) married shortly afterward they began experimenting in fused, enameled, sheet glass—an innovation in art glass. Now in their eighties, they continue to experiment with new forms and techniques. Collectors have discovered what museums have known for years—that their work is of museum quality. Both have always created their own designs. She specializes in jewelry along with decorative pieces. Michael's specialized designs range from bowls to plaques. One of his pieces, a plaque titled "The Medieval Naval Dockyard," is in the Victoria and Albert Museum. A retrospective book of their pieces is in the works.

Through the years they have produced a wide variety of objects from earrings to a 500-square-foot curtain of glass. Their work is a part of many museum collections. They are seeing a revived interest in the work they did many years ago, including early mobiles.

In early experiments they began with clear glass, fusing up to three layers. By 1959 they were using enamels. Their first retail customers were Marshall Fields and C. D. Peacocks in Chicago.

Michael organized the Midwest Designer Craftsmen. In the 1960s they copyrighted their names on their "fused" glass. Many have imitated their work.

Collectors should beware of dealers who buy direct from the Higginses, then sell the pieces as early work, at the correspondingly higher prices.

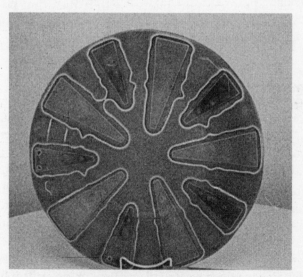

Charger, designed by Michael Higgins, c. 1960s. Beige, orange, tangerine, signed HIGGINS in gold; $200. Courtesy of Decor Moderne.

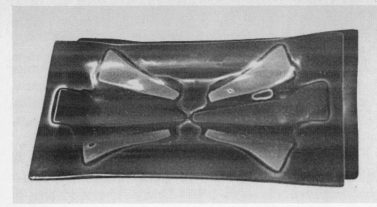

Ashtray, designed by Michael Higgins, c. 1960s. Bright orange and gold, signed HIGGINS with gold symbol; $50. Courtesy of the author.

PRICES

Enameled Glass Platter, designed by Michael Higgins, c. 1970. Clear glass; circular platter with a radiating design in yellow and white, heightened with platinum luster; inscribed "HIGGINS"; 15 inches in diameter; $287.

DOMINICK LABINO (1910–   )

Dominick Labino is recognized as an important technician who invented many processes that led to the studio art glass movement. Among them was his creation of an easy-to-melt glass formula and a portable furnace and annealing oven that allowed the individual production of blown studio glass. At the 1979 Corning Museum of Glass Exhibition, Labino showed a work titled "Triangular Fountain," part of his Immersion series, using the hot-glass techniques he had originally experimented with in the late 1950s. He was among the first to make Expressionist shapes in hot glass, elevating form and color to primary objectives. His glass is essentially furnace work with sculptural form made from the hot glass. The decorative pieces are not cut or etched and then reheated and encased, but are the result of his knowledge of the glassblower's art.

He retired from the industrial aspects of glass production and has spent the past decade perfecting new forms of his glassblowing artistry.

PRICES

Dominick Labino Applied Bowl, 1970. Swirled colorless and red polished glass vessel with four symmetrically manipulated prunts; engraved "LABINO I-D 1970"; 3 inches high × 6 inches in diameter; $1,300.

Dominick Labino Blown-Glass Bowl, 1967. Swirled liquid reactive blue, gold, and red dimpled form; engraved "LABINO 1967"; 3¼ inches × 6¼ inches in diameter; $120.

Three Dominick Labino Glass Tumblers, 1968, 1970. Transparent green swirled with opaque red-opal glass of free-blown design; each signed and dated; 3½ inches to 4 inches high; $550/set.

Three Dominick Labino Blown-Glass Decorations, 1966, 1965, 1964. Swirled opal paperweight with central blue blossom; green transparent double-bulbed tumbler; sapphire-blue inkwell form; each signed and dated; $750/set.

Dominick Labino Bottle Vase, c. 1960. Free-blown aquamarine vessel of great clarity and precision; early work; inscribed "LABINO"; 6¼ inches high; $165.

MARVIN LIPOFSKY (1938–   )

Marvin Lipofsky studied with Harvey Littleton and in 1964 founded the second glass program in America at the University of California at Berkeley. In 1972 it was forced to close due to lack of funding. During the next fifteen years he became head of the glass program at the California College of Arts and Crafts.

He has a B.F.A. from the University of Illinois and an M.S. and M.F.A. from the University of Wisconsin.

His work is in collections of the American Craft Museum,

New York; the Corning Museum of Glass, New York; the Detroit Institute of Arts, Michigan; the Oakland Museum, California; the Arts and Crafts Museum, Prague, Czechoslovakia; the Museum of Contemporary Art, Skopje, Yugoslavia; and the High Museum of Art, Atlanta, Georgia.

PRICES

Holding Series, from Fratelli Toso series, Murano, Italy, 1979. Blown-glass shard; plaster life casting of artist's hand; signed and dated; 10½ inches high × 12 inches long × 7½ inches deep; $6,500.

HARVEY KLINE LITTLETON (1922–   )

Harvey Littleton is probably America's most influential modern studio glass maker. His pieces get top dollar when they come to auction, which is rarely. His background, like the backgrounds of so many important American artisans, includes a stint at Cranbrook Academy, where he studied ceramics. In 1951 he began teaching ceramics at the Toledo Museum of Art, and continued until 1977. However, in 1957 while visiting the glass factories in Europe, he became interested in experimenting with glass. The concept of creating studio glass resulted in a paper presented to the American Craft Council in 1961. He attended experimental workshops held at the Toledo Museum of Art, where instruction was given by Dominick Labino, research director for John S. Manville Fiberglas. After further studies Littleton began teaching glassblowing at the University of Wisconsin, where he began what became the American studio glass movement.

His early work is characterized by Expressionism—using bubbles of glass first imploded, then exploded. Decorative prunts and trails were added. By the end of the 60s he simplified his designs. He used brightly colored glass tubes to form, in essence, sculptures. Currently he continues to experiment with the technical aspects of glass as well as glass forms and colors.

PRICES

Untitled, 1979. Drawn, cut, and polished glass; signed and dated; 12 inches high × 11¾ inches wide; $3,000.

JOEL PHILIP MYERS (1934–   )

Joel Myers designed for Blenko Glass of West Virginia from 1961 to 1970. He established a studio glass program in 1971 at the University of Illinois. Using the warm technique, he did a series called Contiguous Fragments wherein the vessels were free-blown and then, using a glass marquetry technique, decorated. It took him many years to develop this technique. The end result appears as abstract art.

PRICES

Studio Glass Vase, 1967–1969. Free-blown colorless vessel externally decorated by abstract portraiture; inscribed "JOEL PHILIP MEYERS 1967–69"; 10 inches high; $1,540.

THOMAS J. PATTI (1943–   )

Patti is considered to be one of America's leading glass artists. His work is extremely technical, though it appears a simple process. About his own work he has said, "It is integral in my work to force the relationship of art and technology." In comparison with other glass artists his output is relatively small.

He studied with Rudolph Arnheim and Sybil Moholy-Nagy. He earned a degree from Pratt Institute, School of Art and Design, Brooklyn, New York, in 1969. His work is represented in the collections of the Coburg Museum, West Germany; the Philadelphia Museum of Art; the Brockton Art Museum, Massachusetts; the Museum of Modern Art, New York; the Metropolitan Museum of Art, New York; the Corning Museum of Glass, New York; the Lobmeyr Museum, Vienna, Austria; and the Toledo Museum of Art in Ohio.

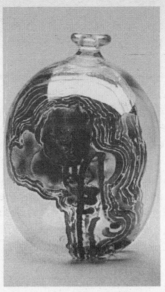

Studio Glass Vase, designed by Joel Philip Meyers. Freeblown colorless vessel externally decorated by abstract portraiture, inscribed JOEL PHILIP MEYERS 1967–69; 10 inches high; $600–800. Courtesy of Skinner Inc., Boston/Bolton, MA.

PRICES

Bronze with Tubated Clear, 1978. Laminated sheet glass; blown, cut, and polished; signed and dated; $2\frac{11}{16}$ inches high × $2\frac{7}{8}$ inches deep × $3\frac{1}{16}$ inches wide; $3,750.

Green with Line and Air Grid, 1977. Laminated sheet glass; blown, cut, and polished; signed and dated; $2\frac{7}{16}$ inches high × $2\frac{5}{8}$ inches deep × 3 inches wide; $4,000.

❋ OTHER AMERICAN GLASS DESIGNS ❋

PRICES

Glass-and-Copper Vase, 1969. Unusual irregular form; glass with trapped air bubbles; signed "ROBERT BARBER, MAY 1969, UNIV. WIS."; 7 inches high; $600.

Glass Sculpture, designed by Tom Patti, c. 1979. $8,250. Courtesy of Butterfield and Butterfield Auctioneers.

William Carlson Perfume Bottle, 1977. Blown, cut, and polished glass; signed and dated; 5½ inches high; $1,400.

Wayne Filo Bird and Serpent Vase, 1975. Flared vessel of colorless glass with silver-overlaid surface applications depicting snakes and long-necked birds; inscribed "WAYNE FILO . . . 1975"; 8 inches high; $275.

Studio Glass Vase, by Michael Harris, Medina Glass, Malta, c. 1968. Rolled rim on bulbous base with trapped geometric composition in colors of sea green and ocher; signed; 6 inches high × 6½ inches in diameter; $125.

Charles Lotton Lava Glass Vase, 1974. Contemporary representation of gold iridescent cased and applied "ancient" glass form; mounted in hand-wrought three-prong gilt metal stand; glass engraved "LOTTON 1979"; 7 inches high; $600.

Mask from Comedia del l'Arte Series, by Gianni Toso, 1979.

Flared Vessel of Colorless Glass, 1975. Silver overlaid surface applications depicting snakes and long-necked birds, inscribed WAYNE FILO . . . *1975; 8 inches high; $275.* Courtesy of Skinner Inc., Boston/ Bolton, MA.

Blown glass; signed and inscribed "PFEIFFER RIDGE STUDIO"; dated; 8 inches × 7 inches; $2,750.

❀ GREAT BRITAIN ❀

It wasn't until after World War II that the way people perceived glass began to change. Up until then, and throughout history, glasswork was considered a craft. Initially its major purpose was functional. While glass was used in an artistic way—consider the stained-glass windows of the Middle Ages, and those made by Louis Comfort Tiffany, with his art glass, along with the work of Gallé and Lalique—making it was still viewed as a craft rather than an art form.

By the 1940s individual European glass artists in Czechoslovakia, Italy, and Scandinavia were experimenting outside the glassworks, creating small sculptural pieces.

In Britain of the 40's there were a rare few studio glass artists. It was engravers such as John Hutton and Laurence Whistler, however, who truly experimented with their techniques, primarily stipple engraving. Another glassblower, Sam Herman, made the first major breakthrough in 1969. He studied with Harvey Littleton before coming to Britain in 1965, on a Fulbright scholarship. When he began teaching at the Royal College of Art in 1969 his use of bold color combinations and dramatic free-blown forms gave a new incentive to the glass movement.

In 1969 he helped found The Glasshouse in London, where for the first time glass students became part of a cooperative.

The London Glassblowing Workshop was founded in 1970 at Rotherhithe in East London by Peter Layton, also a founding member of The Glasshouse. In 1977 the British Artists in Glass (BAG) was started by a small group of British glassmakers.

Some names to look for include David Taylor and Catherine Hough, both known for their scent bottles. Steven Newell (another founding member of The Glasshouse) uses a technique that produces animal or human figure motifs etched or sandblasted onto the surface of the piece, generally bowls and large plates. Pauline Solvens's work shows a Scandinavian influence, but with a striking use of color techniques. Fantasy shapes identify much of the glass sculpture of Stephen Procter.

PRICES

Vase, 1975. Free-blown studio glass made by Samuel J. Herman. Internally decorated incorporating layers of undulating varicolored metal. Inscribed "SAMUEL J. HERMAN 1975"; 6½ inches high; $330.

❋ ITALY ❋

BAROVIER AND TOSO

This Italian glassworks began producing colorful glass in a variety of textures and abstract designs in 1942. Ercole Barovier

(1889–1974) is considered among the important designers of modern glass, along with his son, Angelo Barovier (1927–   ). Their designs used abstract sculptural forms with minute bubbles and spots of color within the glass.

PRICES

Barovier and Toso Glass Vase, c. 1960. Composed of five square section vessels in pale green, gray, amber, and white opalescent cased glass; unsigned; 13¾ inches high; $690.

Barovier and Toso Dorico Vase, designed by Ercole Barovier, c. 1960. Composed of square murrinas in clear, opal, brick-red, and amethyst; unsigned; 5 inches high; mint condition; $4,750.

Barovier and Toso Sidereo Bowl, designed by Ercole Barovier, c. 1966. Clear body overlaid with a network of clear and opaque white rings with applied foot; engraved signature "BAROVIER & TOSO MURANO"; 9 inches in diameter; mint condition; $1,800.

Barovier and Toso Glass Vase, designed by Angelo Barovier, c. 1960. Composed of five square section vessels in pale green, gray, amber, and white opalescent cased glass; unsigned; 13¾ inches high; $690.

Barovier and Toso Graffito Barbarico Opaco Vase, designed by Ercole Barovier, c. 1969. Clear with internal decoration of white striations colored with blue powders enclosing large air bubbles and a fine layer of gold; 9 inches high; mint condition; $70.

Barovier and Toso Christian Dior Bottle, designed by Ercole Barovier, c. 1969. Clear with a tartan design in red, blue, green, white, and amethyst with a blue stopper; engraved signature "CHRISTIAN DIOR"; 9½ inches high; mint condition; $11,000.

FULVIO BIANCONI (1915–   )

Fulvio Bianconi is regarded as one of the most important Italian glass designers of the postwar years, when he began designing

---

Intarsio Vase, designed by Ercole Barovier for Barovier & Toso, c. 1961. Composited of light amber and brilliant red triangular patches cased with a clear layer; 10½ inches high × 10½ inches in diameter; $2,400. Courtesy of Toomey-Treadway Galleries, Oak Park, IL.

perfume bottles and graphics. His meeting in 1948 with Paolo Venini resulted in Bianconi's joining the Venini glasshouse. The humorous figurines of commedia del l'arte characters were designed by Bianconi for Venini. Other postwar designs now considered among his finest were the handkerchief vase and later his Scottish vases featuring plaids of caning. In the 1960s he worked for Vitossi, collaborating on designs. One such piece, a vase with spiral stripes, won an award at the Milan XIII Triennale of 1964. His work of the 1970s included a series of heads and glass cubes with figures drawn in glass that are encased within. The pieces of this later period have a sculptural quality.

PRICES

Venini and C. Sculpture, designed by Fulvio Bianconi. Combines Mask and Patchwork series; gentleman composed of

---

black mask face, hat, trousers, shoes, opaque white latimo hair, beard, collar, stockings, and gloves with four fingers on the right hand and five fingers on the left; his coat is transparent red, blue, green pezzato squares; stamped on base "VENINI MUR-ANO, ITALIA"; 14 inches high; $3,575.

Fulvio Bianconi Vase, for Cenedese, attribution. Two walls of red-and-white glass with abstract Jackson Pollock–style splatter decoration; 12 inches high × 5 inches in diameter; mint condition; $450.

CARLO SCARPA (1906–1978)

Not only was Carlo Scarpa one of Italy's foremost mid-twentieth-century architects and industrial designers, he was also a multifaceted designer of glass, furniture, and flatware. Some of his finest glass designs were done in the 1940s for Venini glassworks. During those years he designed the Tessuto series, which used a ground with cane patterns. He also created the Battuto series in the 40s, with a ground surface that looked like beaten metal. Before leaving Venini in 1947, he designed pieces using irregular splashes of colored glass wound around simple shapes.

Over the years he designed small accessories and furniture for his clients and himself. In the 1960s and 1970s he devoted most of his time to this pursuit. Many of his designs for silver, some originally produced for Reed and Barton, were adapted and produced in 1976 by the Italian firm of Rossi and Arcandi.

Some of his most outstanding works include:

- Doge table in steel and glass, 1968.
- Orseolo writing table in treated wood and black lacquer, 1973.
- Toledo range of beds in turned wood with leather headboards, 1975.
- Cutlery set in gold and silver for Cleto Munari, 1977–1978.

Venini Corroso Bowl, designed by Carlo Scarpa, c. 1933. Green cased over blue with a corroso (acid-etched) surface and an iridescent interior; acid-stamped "VENINI MURANO, MADE IN ITALY"; 4¼ inches in diameter; mint condition; $700.

ARCHIMEDE SEGUSO (1909–)

Born in the glassmaking city of Murano, Italy, Archimede Seguso is considered one of the ultimate glassblowers. He began blowing glass at the age of thirteen. By 1929 he began making his own items using a small furnace in the family fireplace. His professional life began when he and others founded Seguso Vetri d'Arte in 1934, and he acted as master glassblower. In 1947 he founded his own company, Vetreria Archimede Seguso. After the war he became known for his variations of the traditional Venetian latticino glass, among them his "lace" and "feather" vases. Many of his creations were for the tabletop, but he also created sculptures and chandeliers. He continues his work today.

PRICES

Archimede Seguso Glass Center Bowl, c. 1960. Irregular vessel in clear glass internally decorated with purple and rose shadings and gold foil inclusions; unsigned; 12⅝ inches long; $230.

Archimede Seguso Opaline Shell, c. 1962. Opaline cased over yellow; 8 inches long; mint condition; $80.

Archimede Seguso Opaline Vase, c. 1961. Opal shaded to deep red; 13¼ inches high; mint condition; $500.

Archimede Seguso Grillwork Vase. Sparkling flattened oval vessel of green amber striped and ridged transparent glass; 12¼ inches high; $990.

Archimede Seguso Opaline Lemon, c. 1963. Opaque yellow

body with colorless leaf and stem; paper label reads "MADE IN MURANO ITALY"; 6½ inches long; mint condition; $100.

VENINI S.p.A.

One of the most familiar names for collectors of Modern glass, the Venini glassworks, had its beginnings in 1921. Paolo Venini (1895–1959), a Milanese lawyer, formed a company with an antiques dealer from the family of glassblowers and Andrea Rhoda, a Venetian glassmaker. The partnership ended in 1925, after they had jointly created prize-winning glassware. Paolo Venini formed a new company that created humorous animals and potted plants until 1931. After the war, in 1946, Gio Ponti and, later, in 1948, Fulvio Bianconi designed the stylized Modern pieces that are eagerly sought by collectors today. Among them are a series of bottles with anthropomorphic shapes, the handkerchief bowls, biomorphic vases, and stylized figural bottles. After the death of Paolo Venini, his widow and son-in-law, Ludovico de Santilla, introduced new artists to the company. Tobia Scarpa, son of architect Carlo Scarpa, was among them.

In the 1960s Venini employed the talents of American Thomas Stearns. However, his use of dark colors wasn't popular. In 1966, 1970, and 1972 the Finnish designer Tapio Wirkkala did many designs in the Venini style. American studio glass artists, including Dale Chihuly, James Carpenter, and others, also did designs at the factory.

Venini is reproducing many of the 40s, 50s, and 60s classics. Included are the commedia del l'arte figures (clowns, for example), handkerchief vases, and bottles. While some of the figures weren't signed, collectors are advised to become familiar with the variety of signatures and paper labels. The auction catalog "Important Italian Glass," published for the November 15, 1992, specialized auction at John Toomey Gallery in Oak Park, Illinois, shows not only important glassware and prices but also various Venini signatures. The catalog is available through Ripley's Antique Galleries, 1502 West McCarty Street, Indianapolis, IN 46221, for $45.

Mezza Filigrana Bowl. Composed of pale amber stripes alternating with brown and white latticino ribbons; stamped "VENINI MURANO ITALIA"; $3\frac{3}{4}$ inches high × $5\frac{3}{4}$ inches long; $220.

Two Venini Glass Vases, designed by Pierre Cardin, c. 1968. In two sizes; each square in azure blue glass decorated with a random stripe of yellow; each inscribed "VENINI PIERRE CARDIN"; heights are $7\frac{3}{4}$ inches and $4\frac{5}{8}$ inches; $1,150.

Sculptural Vase, designed by Pierre Cardin, c. 1968. Clear rectangular form block; open at the bottom with a layer of opaque bright orange slumped over the top forming four open drops; 10 inches high × 4 inches deep × $9\frac{1}{2}$ inches wide; mint condition; $2,600.

Venini Glass Centerpiece, probably designed by Toni Zuccheri, c. 1966. Irregular form in olive-green glass cased within corrugated clear glass and molded with deep ridges resembling a large cabbage leaf; inscribed "VENINI/ITALIA"; 18 inches in diameter; $920.

Two Venini Glass Decanters, c. 1962. Each of squared bottle form; one in marine blue glass decorated with deep cobalt raised concentric trailing and flattened domical blue glass stopper; the second in bottle-green glass decorated with hot orange raised concentric trailing with conforming flattened domical stopper; inscribed "VENINI/ITALIA"; the first acid-stamped "VENINI/MURANO/ITALIA"; heights: $8\frac{3}{4}$ inches and 9 inches, respectively; $2,587.

Fish, designed by Ken Scott, c. 1966. Hollow body of smoky amethyst with applied yellow and orange stripes; blue eye with internal white pupil and black mouth; engraved signature "VENINI ITALIA"; 15 inches long; $4,000.

Thomas Stearns Venini Vase, c. 1965. Cylindrical form of colorless glass; uncalmo technique applied spiral decoration at top; opaque purple iridescent band at bottom; 10 inches high × 4 inches in diameter; mint condition; $4,000.

Beverage Set, designed by Fulvio Bianconi, c. 1960. Venini fasce vertical fused canes of smoky gray and opaque white, acid-stamped VENINI MURANO ITALIA, *includes pitcher and four tumblers; $425.* Courtesy of Toomey-Treadway Galleries, Oak Park, IL.

Glass Vase, designed by Thomas Stearns, c. 1962. Cylindrical vessel in clear glass decorated with spiral threading in gunmetal and violet above a deep brick-red base; unsigned; retains original paper label; 9½ inches high; $2,875.

❋ OTHER ITALIAN GLASS DESIGNS ❋

PRICES

AVEM Glass Vase, c. 1960. Flattened elongated vessel with irregular rim; in clear glass decorated with a pattern of squares in blue, yellow, green, and red among a field of white and green canes; unsigned; 20¼ inches high; $4,312.

Cendese Bowl, c. 1963. Free-blown chartreuse-green, transparent vessel with wide band of enclosed murrine decoration in amethyst, bright turquoise, and dark green; very optical; 6 inches high × 8 inches in diameter; mint condition; $450.

Bookends, c. 1960. Cenedese, freeform, green glass with internal dark green patches and applied block feet; 8¼ inches high; $160. Courtesy of Toomey-Treadway Galleries, Oak Park, IL.

Gino Cendese Cased Swirl Bowl. Colorless glass cased to white with internal pink, green, amber, and blue alternating with yellow stripes in diagonal swirl design; engraved "CEN-DESE" on base; 6½ inches high × 9½ inches in diameter; $350.

Flavio Poli Glass Centerpiece, c. 1960. Palest amethyst glass; oval vessel raised on a thick circular foot; unsigned; 4⅞ inches high × 15½ inches long; $230.

Salviati figure modeled as a pig, probably designed by Luciano Gaspari, c. 1965. Solid clear body with sommerso layers of yellow and red; unsigned; 6½ inches long; mint condition; $325.

Murano Glass for Knoll Associates, c. 1960s. Two red glass mushroom vases; heights 6 inches and 4 inches; mint condition; $100/set.

Large Murano Bowl and Underplate, probably c. 1970. Opaque red interiors cased in black; the bowl allowing for red external patches; cased in clear glass; paper label reads "MADE IN ITALY"; 7 inches high × 19½ inches wide; mint condition; $600.

Murano Sommerso Polar Bear Figure, probably by Salviati, c. 1965. Solid clear body with internal core of green; 10 inches long; mint condition; $210.

Murano Sommerso Pitcher Form, probably Seguso Vetri d'Arte. Layers of clear, yellow, cobalt blue, and red; unsigned; 13 inches high; mint condition; $600.

Large Murano Sommerso Vase, probably Salviati, c. 1960. Solid translucent aqua-green body with internal blue layer; unsigned; 21 inches high; mint condition; $1,100.

Large Murano Sommerso Obelisk, probably Venini. Solid amber with internal dark core; unsigned; 24¾ inches high; mint condition; $2,750.

Salviati Figure, c. 1965. Modeled as a chicken; transparent lime-green body, amethyst tail and face, and yellow beak; opaque red comb; white eye and clear base; paper label reads "SAVIATI & C., MADE IN ITALY"; 7¾ inches high; mint condition; $85.

Seguso Vetri d'Arte Glass Vase, designed by Flavio Poli, c. 1960. Large flattened flaring cylindrical vessel in transparent orange glass; unsigned; 19 inches high; $1,150.

Two Vistosi Glass Vases, designed by Dino Martins, c. 1960s. First is of waisted cylindrical form in orange iridescent glass decorated at the waist with alternating blue and red glass canes; second is of double conical form with elongated cylindrical neck in turquoise iridescent glass decorated at the shoulder with blue, green, and turquoise canes; both unsigned; 9¼ inches and 11 inches high, respectively; $1,150.

❊ SCANDINAVIA ❊

KOSTA GLASBRUK

The oldest Swedish glassworks, still in existence, Kosta was founded in 1741. In the beginning they made drinking glasses, chandeliers, and windowpanes. By the end of the nineteenth century they produced cameo glass in the manner of Emile Gallé. In 1950 the factory hired prominent designer Vicke Lindstrand, who had previously worked at the Orrefors factory. He created the asymmetrical forms that became popular after World War II.

Glass Vase, c. 1960. Brown and white loops on white, paper label marked ARDULT, AA, MADE IN ITALY; *9½ inches high; $150.* Courtesy of The Time Machine.

Many Scandinavian glass pieces, notably those from Finland and Sweden, were not literally made by the designer but by a master engraver or master glassblower.

ULRICA HYDMAN-VALLIEN (1938–   )

Married to one of the great glass artists, Bertil Vallien, Ulrica Hydman-Vallien is an artist whose works can be recognized by their distinctive painted designs of her own fantasy. Her background was in ceramics, and she studied first at the National College of Arts and Design in Stockholm from 1958 to 1961, followed by two years of study in Mexico and the United States. She met Bertil Vallien when both were students in their native Sweden. In 1972 she became a free-lance designer and created many pieces for Kosta Boda. Her technique combines sandblasting, etching, and painting on an underlay and overlay

Goblet, Artist's Collection, Kosta Boda, #98821. Pale blue bowl with yellow cat head with the word "dear," pale pink stem, blue foot, signed with the initials U.H.V., (even though this was done in the early 1980s, it typifies Ulrica Hydman-Vallien's style); $150. Courtesy of the author.

of crystal glass in a variety of colors. She has designed both functional pieces and sculpture.

KAJ FRANCK (1911–)

Kaj Franck is a multifaceted designer of Finnish glass, furniture, textiles, ceramics, and interiors. He studied interior design from 1929 to 1932 at the Institute of Industrial Arts, Helsinki, Finland. Among the many companies he designed for, beginning in 1933, were Taito Oy, Riihimaki Glass, Wollfabriken, Wartsila-Arabia, and Wartsila-Nuutajarvi glassworks. From 1960 to 1967 he was the artistic director of the Institute of Industrial Arts, Helsinki. After his retirement in 1976 he worked as a free-lance designer and international lecturer. His works are in collections in Finland's Glassmuseum, Helsinki;

the Museum of Applied Arts, Helsinki; the Victoria and Albert Museum, London; the Corning Glass Museum, Corning, New York; and others. His notable designs include:

- Facet glassware for Nuutajarvi, 1962
- Prisma glassware for Nuutajarvi, 1967
- Delfoi glassware for Nuutajarvi, 1978
- Easy Day plastic tableware and cutlery for Sarvas, 1979
- Teema earthenware kitchen and table service ranges for Arabia, 1979–1981

VIKTOR EMANUEL (VICKE) LINDSTRAND (1904–1983)

Vicke Lindstrand is one of Sweden's most famous glass designers. His avant-garde designs were recognized as early as 1935, at an important Stockholm exhibition. As a designer for Orrefors Glasbruk, he initially produced designs in the Modern classicism style. In the 1940s his vases with nudes were influenced by Matisse, while those with animals were more abstract. In 1950 he became artistic director at Kosta Glasbruk, where he remained until his retirement in 1971.

His works have been exhibited worldwide and are in private collections as well as represented in the permanent collections of the Victoria and Albert Museum, London; the Louvre, Paris; the Metropolitan Museum of Art, New York; and others.

The forms of his vases were asymmetric, and he used internal color threads. In the late 50s he used a thicker crystal. Many of his vases are biomorphic, some with shallow holes on one side. It wasn't until 1964 that he began designing glass sculptures.

PRICES

Kosta Glass Vase, designed by Vicke Lindstrand, c. 1965. Swollen flattened cylindrical vessel in clear glass internally decorated with pale blue vertical trailings; acid-stamped "LIND/ STRAND/KOSTA"; inscribed "LH 205-4081"; $690.

Orrefors Swedish Bubble Vase, designed by Vicke Lindstrand. Crystal sphere centrally engraved with naked child blowing polished bubble seen around and through the bowl; inscribed; signed and numbered "1382 E 3KR"; $220.

ORREFORS GLASBRUK AB

Founded in 1726 in the Swedish province of Amaland, Orrefors was at first an ironworks. It wasn't until 1913 that the company hired skilled workers and began producing cameo glass. Over the years Orrefors established a reputation for quality engraved glass. In postwar Sweden, Nils Landberg created designs in the Modern manner. Especially noteworthy are his Tulip goblets. They were blown from a single pull of glass, with thin, elongated stems. Of cased glass, they used gradations of colors. Another important glass designer employed at Orrefors was Ingeborg Lundin.

PRICES

Two Swedish Art Glass Vases. Blue netted design by Sven Palmquist, with colorless shaded to blue crystal, inscribed "ORREFORS PU3367" and signed, 8 inches high; attributed to Beng and Edenfalk, colorless crystal bowl with controlled bubble motif, $3\frac{7}{8}$ inches high; $440/set.

TAPIO WIRKKALA (1915–1985)

Wirkkala was a famed industrial designer and sculptor whose influential works continued until 1984. His career began in the postwar era when Scandinavian design was dominant. He studied sculpture at the School of Industrial Arts in Helsinki in his native Finland. From 1946 to 1985 he was a glass designer for Karhula-litala. He was also the founder and director of Tapio Wirkkala Design Studio, Helsinki, which he formed in 1955. His work in glass and laminated wood serving pieces won many

---

Orrefors Crystal Sculpture. Narrow, swirled colorless glass block molded with concave circles at front and back, inscribed ORREFORS EXPO P787-72 SVEN PALMQUIST; 9¾ inches high × 2⅛ inches deep × 8 inches wide; $302.50. Courtesy of Skinner Inc., Boston/Bolton, MA.

Orrefors Ariel Vase, c. 1960s. Heavy walled crystal internally decorated with trapped air bubble design, blue and yellow striations, inscribed ORREFORS KRAKA N.411 SVEN PALMQUIST; $357.50. Courtesy of Skinner Inc., Boston/Bolton, MA.

Orrefors Ariel Vase, designed by Ingeborg Lundin, c. 1970. Internal geometric decoration of trapped air bubbles and blue with a light amber layers, engraved ORREFORS ARIEL NO. 405-E INGEBORG LUNDIN; 9½ inches high; $1,500. Courtesy of Toomey-Treadway Galleries, Oak Park, IL.

awards over the years. He was hired as an industrial designer to create products in ceramics, silver, glass, and wood.

❋ CZECHOSLOVAKIA ❋

In the 1940s and 1950s many of the top Czech artists not only designed but created art glass. It took an exhibit at the 1957 Milan Triennale and another at the Brussels World Fair of 1958 to expose the unique talents of Czech glass artists and their contribution to the Modern movement in the rest of the world.

Littala Lasithedas Vase, designed by Tapio Wirkkala, c. 1960s. Clear with internal layer of deep amethyst and large rising air bubble in bottom, engraved TAPIO WIRKKALA-3856; 11 inches high; $210. Courtesy of Toomey-Treadway Galleries, Oak Park, IL.

Smoked Glass Bowl and Two Vases, designed by Per Lutken for Holmegaard, Denmark, signed, c. 1960s. $150/each. Courtesy of Decor Moderne.

Czech art glass differed from other Modern styles in its use of enameling and other surface techniques. Toward the end of the 50s Czech artists were influenced by the growing interest in abstract paintings and used brightly colored enamels in abstract patterns.

Czech glass designs began to influence Western artists in the 1960s, despite the fact that the artists worked in practical isolation from the West. It was a glass collage, executed by René Roubicek, winner of the Grand Prix at Expo 58 in Brussels, that caught the attention of glass artists in the West. Roubicek developed novel techniques with his blown glass. He is still working and innovating with glass sculpture. This is the path most Czech artists followed in the 70s. Through various exhibits and symposiums, and more recently the changed political climate of Czechoslovakia, both artists and collectors are getting acquainted.

Stanislav Libensky (1921–), one of the early influentials in Czech studio glass, began teaching painting on glass at Novy Bor, the Czech glassmaking school, in 1945. His work was influenced by such painters as Antonio Tapies and early Renaissance artists. By 1955 he worked in conjunction with his wife, Jaroslava Brychrova, a sculptor. Their early pieces were produced on a massive scale that included stained-glass windows and large sculptures such as the *River of Life*, done for Expo 70 in Osaka, Japan. Libensky combined industrial design with his career as a glass artist. He is mentioned here not only for his monumental works of great influence but also for his smaller, collectible pieces.

Pavel Hlava (1924–) has always pioneered new blown-glass techniques, and has also worked in large scale.

René Roubicek (1922–) used glass as if it were crystal. This artist's sculptural, carved pieces used in-depth relief cutting. The resultant figures look similar to stone carvings.

Vladimir Kopecky (1931–) developed a distinctive technique that uses glass as a painter uses canvas. His heavy use of enamels forms patterns on the glass. He has also produced sculpture with the effect of three-dimensional paintings.

Other artists to look for include Jiri Harcuba (1928–) and Miluse Roubickova.

Because these artists and their works are relatively unknown to the average dealer or collector, there are bargains to be found. Unlike the glass of Scandinavia and Italy, Czech art glass rarely comes to auction. When it does, prices are often on the low side.

Graphics

✸ POSTERS

George Theofiles, who founded Miscellaneous Man, a vintage graphics firm, in 1970, specializes in posters and graphic memorabilia. He prides himself on handling no reproductions or reprints. His interest in posters began at age eight, with the purchase of his first work: "I Want You For The U.S. Army." He has gone on to become an all-around expert in a growing field. He advises that "vintage collectibles are a tough business to learn." He generously gives advice on preservation and history to beginning collectors who contact him in New Freedom, Pennsylvania.

Movie posters have always been the basic influence for everything from 1940s war propaganda to fashion. The purpose and the look of the art poster have changed since the late 1930s, when posters often featured slogans. Patriotic poster imagery of the 40s and recruitment propaganda were key subjects. Famed French artist Jean Carlu, who had been doing war propaganda posters for the French government, was in America when the war broke out and stayed here, where he did posters. Famous American illustrators such as Steven Dohanos and Norman Rockwell donated their talents for small fees. One of the most famous is the four-freedoms series. Millions were produced. Currently any single poster from the series would be around $100.

During World War II Switzerland was neutral. It was here that several important poster artists did object posters for the first time, among them Hans Falk and Otto Baumberger. PKZ men's clothing posters were clean and crisp. These sell from $150 to several thousand dollars. At the same time the Swiss magazine

Graphis offered a monthly poster to subscribers.

In the late 40s some of the best posters were done for the New York subway by Paul Rand. Other ads were influenced by the new social mores of the upper and middle classes. Rand's works are considered rare since only a thousand or so were printed. They sell for $500 and up.

Art exhibit posters, even those promoting Léger and Matisse, are not expensive. They were made to be sold as souvenirs, for the first time in the 1950s. Today they sell for from $5 to $25. From 1949 to 1959 the Gallery Maeght in Paris produced most of the art exhibition posters.

There are few posters from the "Beatnik" era worth looking for. The Jack Kerouac book posters were popular in the 50s. However, they were taped on walls and treated casually. In the end most were destroyed. They would sell for several hundred dollars today.

The 1950s saw the development of dance groups and small theater companies such as that of Lee Strasberg. The posters made to promote them are interesting for their documentary messages. They are rare.

Transportation posters from the 50s range from $100 to $300. In the growing air travel business, airlines such as Pan Am competed with the steamships, so many of their posters are graphically appealing. Look for those by American artists. Railroad posters that are very desirable are those done by Leslie Reagan and Grif Teller.

In the 1950s Spanish bullfight posters became a cultural icon and over sixty thousand were sold for a few dollars. Today they have no particular value for collectors and sell for around $5 each.

Posters of the 60s were silk screened and sold in stores. There were the Op, Hippie, and antiwar message posters. Generally these American posters sell for around $150. The French student revolt of 1968 was done on poor newsprint, so few have survived. They sell for between $250 and $300.

Important psychedelic posters were done by Victor Moscosco, Stanley Mouse, Wes Wilson, and Rick Griffin. There have been reproductions of early 60s posters as far back as 1967. The most popular reproduction is "Woodstock." Collectors should note that the original is 24 inches × 36 inches while the reproduction is smaller. The original sells for $500 to $700 at auction, for $1,500 in galleries.

Thousands of rock posters were made and left unsold. However, while the majority sell for as little as $10, some, such as an early Grateful Dead, could sell for $1,500.

"The poster market is bullish, whether old or new," according to Palm Beach dealers Robert Perrin and Peter Langlykke of Poster Graphics Inc. They suggest that collectors of 60s and 70s posters seek out travel and automobile subjects, which currently are "sleepers." They also advise putting posters of famous places or buildings that no longer exist away for the future. Other frequently overlooked categories are benefit and advertising posters that have graphic merit. An example would be the poster done by Alexander Girard for Herman Miller Textiles. It would offer good graphics and the added benefit of a top-name designer and graphic artist.

"Most people don't know what to do with posters when

they get dog-eared, so they throw them away," said Perrin. "Yet often they can be restored by putting linen backing on them."

"If I were a collector I'd go to auto dealers to look for their old posters," suggested Langlykke. "Racing posters, such as the auto races from LeMans and Monaco, have exciting graphics and are also worth putting away. After all, just four years ago the Robert Indiana "Love" poster retailed for $25. Now, if you can find one, it would sell for $1,000."

Prices are based on many factors, among them the artist and availability of a particular piece.

❀ BLACK MOVIE POSTERS ❀

The current collector interest in early movie posters has unearthed a new collecting speciality, black movie posters. John Kisch, author and collector, and fellow collector Edward Mapp, who have documented their history in *A Separate Cinema—Fifty Years of Black Cast Posters*, are largely responsible. Kisch has been searching for examples since 1972.

"Black images and performers in the movies are nothing new: they have been an integral part of American cinema almost from its beginning," Kisch notes. "In some respects, early black movie history falls into two distinct categories, with two vastly different perspectives and identities. On one side are the race movies; on the other side are the independent filmmakers, some black, others white, who sought to provide mass entertainment for a black audience by creating stories with distinct cultural references, signs, and signposts; by dramatizing worlds in which African-American heroes and heroines were depicted as vital, ambitious, assertive protagonists. Then we have the images and performers that reached audiences by way of Hollywood."

Black movie posters reflected the changes in attitudes of black and white American society. In the 60s and 70s there were films dealing with racial tensions and problems of inner-city life. Such films are, of course, still being made. From a

Black movie poster, Putney Swope, *c. 1969. Black and white; 27 × 41 inches; $100.* Courtesy of Separate Cinema.

collector's point of view, posters for these films are bargains that document troubled decades. Prices range from $20 to around $100.

PRICES

Dorothy Dandridge, *Portrait in Black Holloway House,* 1970, 250 pages; and *Lena Horne Pocket Celebrity Scrapbook,* 1955, 68 pages, 4 inches × 6 inches; Pocket Magazines Inc.; scarce; both mint condition; $50/set.

Muhammad Ali—The Greatest, Columbia Pictures, 1977. Ali shown in full-color design; 28 inches × 22 inches; mint condition; $95.

Muhammad Ali—AKA Cassius Clay, United Artists, 1970. Film poster for *I'm the Greatest Motion Picture Ever Made!,* news photo of Ali in ring; 28 inches × 22 inches; mint condition; $100.

❋ PETER MAX ❋

Probably no one is more symbolic of the art of the 60s and 70s than Peter Max. This European-born artist grew up with a pancultural background in such diverse places as Israel, Tibet, and France. From these influences he developed a linear style of painting using bold color contrasts that are cartoonlike. Though Max began as a Pop artist in the 60s, his style evolved during the 1970s as he embraced various popular causes from the peace movement to the environment. Indeed, the Dove and Love posters of 1969 made him the most popular artist of "The Age of Aquarius." Since 1967 he has been putting his colorful designs on clothes, games, and even cereal boxes and jewelry. To say he is a prolific artist is an understatement, considering the quantities of mass-produced merchandise and limited-edition prints he has created. Yet when collectors go looking for examples they have a hard time.

Probably the most important collection assembled belongs to Larry T. Clemons, who until recently was a dealer specializing in Max items in his Fort Lauderdale, Florida, museum and gallery, Peace on the Planet. Clemons was first exposed to Max at the age of twelve when he first saw the Dove and Love posters. Ever since he has been "putting every penny I ever made into Peter Max art and objects." Clemons also points out that that Love poster sold over three million copies. "Today a rare signed one can sell for over $3,000." Originally the posters sold for between $2 and $10.

Clemons also noted that Peter Max contributes millions of dollars a year to environmental and humanitarian causes, among them a division of his company, AMX, called Global Works, that funds environmental issues.

From a collector's standpoint his work can be categorized thematically. There are examples with peace and environmen-

Peter Max Low-top sneakers. Label on back: HI RANDY; *$500.* Courtesy of Larry Clemmons Collection.

Peter Max Pins (four), c. 1970. Heavy metal and enamel with variety of motifs, made in West Germany, paper label; $150. Courtesy of Larry Clemmons Collection.

tal themes as well as aesthetic nudes and profiles with Matisse-inspired linear elegance and whimsy.

Just entering the United States from Mexico or Canada is an introduction to Max's work. His murals were placed at border crossings in 1978 and will remain under a twenty-year government contract until 1998. His current works are exhibited from time to time around the country and are offered in galleries in New York, Aspen, Palm Beach, and Detroit.

❊ POP ART ❊

Along with the revolutionary changes in design and fashion came a new era in art—the age of Pop Art. As Abstract Expressionism neared its end in the late 50s, new names and art techniques emerged. In the mid-50s artists such as Jasper Johns and Robert Rauschenberg were changing the face of art. Johns's central images were the American flag and targets,

Peter Max Clocks (three). Plastic, two are table clocks; table clocks: $150/ each, round clock: $250. Courtesy of Larry Clemmons Collection.

Peter Max Tote Bags. Plastic, made in Japan; $24/each. Courtesy of Decades.

while Rauschenberg experimented with painting like his *Coca-Cola Plan*, in which images of Coke bottles form the central subject.

Yet another approach that attracted serious art collectors was geometric abstraction. Its artist advocates included Frank Stella, Jasper Johns, and Robert Indiana. Today the Love poster, with the letters of the word forming both the subject and the design, is widely sought by poster collectors. It is a reproduction of the Robert Indiana painting.

Indiana contemporary Jess Collins was making collages that he referred to as "paste-ups" using Dick Tracy comic strips from the color pages of the Sunday comics. Pop Art can be described as making the ordinary into art.

Pop Art was growing in England as well. A group of artists, architects, critics, and historians, known as the Independent Group, were studying the new Pop concepts in every aspect of society. Among them were artists Richard Hamilton and Eduardo Paolozzi, who began doing Pop-style collages in the early 50s. Around the same time another young painter, Peter Blake, began making collages that later evolved into collage image paintings with entertainment figures as central subjects. One of his most notable, titled *Got a Girl* (1960–1961), used a strip of images of contemporary American singers that included Elvis and Ricky Nelson.

In Europe, Pop artists initially referred to themselves as the "New Realists," and their work was introduced to Americans with an exhibit in the Sidney Janis Gallery in New York in 1962. Probably the best known today is Christo. He gained his fame by wrapping found objects in a variety of materials that included canvas, cloth, and plastic. On a humongous scale, he wrapped Florida's Biscayne Bay in miles of pink plastic.

Roy Lichtenstein, now referred to as the "Prince of Pop," transformed the look of the comic strip with its bright, bold colors and balloon text into a new, collectible art.

With his canvases of comic book characters, Roy Lichtenstein helped launch the Pop Art movement. As a serious artist he studied in 1940 at the Art Student League with artist Reginald Marsh, who himself was a major art influence with his scenes of the "ash can school" New York City life. By 1951 Lichtenstein had his first solo exhibit, which reflected his involvement with the then-popular Abstract Expressionist movement.

His early Pop paintings of kitchen appliances and consumer products were modeled on the printed reproductions of the products that appeared in newspaper and magazine ads or even in the yellow pages of the telephone directory. His Pop paintings were first shown at the New York Gallery of Leo Castelli, who also represented Andy Warhol, Claes Oldenburg, and other Pop artists.

Since the 1960s he has also produced posters and sculptures.

Andy Warhol's soup cans and repeat-image art with such subjects as Marilyn Monroe were yet another approach to what was becoming high art in the 60s.

Pop sculpture wasn't embraced as fully as painting and collages in the early 60s. Two of the most prominent Pop sculp-

Work on Canvas: Girl at Piano, *by Roy Lichtenstein; $1,815,000.*
Courtesy of Sotheby's Inc.

tors were painter Claes Oldenburg and Marisol Escobar, who
had left Paris for New York in 1950. Two of Oldenburg's best-
known pieces are his "soft pay telephone" of 1963 and his "bed-
room ensemble" of the same year.

Pop sculpture took on a new appearance with the use of
the new plastic materials. In the 70s, John de Andrea and Duane
Hanson became known as photorealist sculptors. Instead of
using the usual medium of plastic, they chose to work with
polyvinyl, cast vinyl, polyester resin, fiberglass, and polyester.

While these original masterpieces of Pop can sell for millions, there are several options open to the collector with limited funds. The first would be to collect posters that are photo
offset reproductions of the paintings.

Many lesser known artists embodied the Pop look in collages. They often turn up at auction for a few hundred dollars.

Since the 60s and 70s were periods of intense creativity, there are examples of sculpture, both American and international, signed by names you've never heard of. There may well be sleepers among them—artists who became well known in the eighties but worked anonymously in the Pop decades. It is up to you as a collector to familiarize yourself with them. Examine a piece you like and then look up the artist. Many of these artists exhibited at art fairs that proliferated in those decades.

Finally, there are the do-it-yourself craftspeople who experimented with painting, collages, and sculpture. One of my friends fooled visitors for years with her rendition of a Frank Stella oil, which still hangs on her wall. If it ever comes to market as an unsigned piece, it could easily fool a collector. There are many such efforts that are certainly considered Pop Art. They are fun to use as decorative art as long as you don't spend too much money.

The following are prices and examples of affordable, well-known Pop artists' works—and of some unusual do-it-yourself pieces.

ALEXANDER GIRARD (1907–)

Trained as an architect, Girard distinguished himself in all areas of design, including graphics, interiors, furniture, industrial design, and textiles. Many of his bold, colorful designs have been influenced by his collection of folk art.

He opened his first architectural office in Florence, Italy, in 1930 and devoted himself primarily to furnishings and interiors. He returned to America, and Detroit, in 1937. In the 1940s he designed interiors for the Lincoln and Ford motor companies. In 1952 he became design director of the Herman Miller textile division. In 1967 he designed the Girard Group furniture range for Herman Miller Inc.

MILTON GLASER (1929–)

This graphic artist made use of a variety of styles and techniques, often adopted from Art Nouveau and Japanese wood-

Poster, designed by Alexander Girard for Herman Miller Company, 1961. Advertisement, "Textiles and Objects," May 22, 1966, various typographical styles used to promote the new in 1900's motif, red, blue, black, and white; 26 inches × 20 inches; $120. Courtesy Toomey-Treadway Galleries, Oak Park, IL.

cuts. In the end, however, his borrowed styles and techniques fit perfectly with his own bold colors and flat, patterned stylized images. He made decorative lettering a part of many of his posters.

After graduating in 1951 from Cooper Union, where he studied art, he entered the Accademia delle Belle Arti e Liceo Artistico in Bologna, Italy, on a Fulbright scholarship.

By the mid-60s he was commissioned by the music and entertainment industries to design posters.

He contributed art to *Push Pin* graphic magazine in the 60s, and in 1968 he began publishing *New York Magazine* with Clay S. Felker.

*T*extile. Bedspread, Magnum, c. 1970s, close up and view of room. *Courtesy of Jack Lenor Larsen.*

*W*all covering. Shown in period furnished room, 1960s, "Oh Promised Land! Oh Sweet Freedom!" by Jack Denst Designs, Inc. *Courtesy of Jack Denst Designs, Inc.*

Furniture Grouping. Easy Edges, designed by Frank Gehry, consisting of two chairs, two stools and table, laminated cardboard; $4,950. *Courtesy Christie's New York.*

Desk, Table, and Storage Unit, designed by Wendel Castle, 1976. Four of six chairs, laminated and carved maple, signed and dated; $72,000.
Courtesy of Wendel Castle.

Miniature room of a 1970s library, 1970s, created and owned by Ruby and Louis Arkow; $2,500.
Courtesy of Ruby and Louis Arkow.

Furniture and accessories grouping, c. 1960s. Molded lucite, Daffodil chair with upholstered red foam cushion, manufactured by Laverne Originals, New York (other items listed elsewhere); chair: $900.
Courtesy of Fat Chance.

*S*culpture, c. 1970s. "After the Ball," designed by Ruby Arkow, lucite rods, glass, acrylic glue; $200.
Courtesy of Ruby S. and Louis D. Arkow Collection

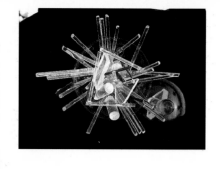

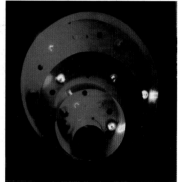

*L*ighting. Psychedelic, outdoor lights, designed for the Woodstock concert, plastic with flashing, rotating lights; $300.
Courtesy of Skank World.

*S*culpture, c. 1960s. Wall sculpture, mixed media, metal and plastic; $350.
Courtesy of Skank World.

*B*ookends (pair), c. 1960s. Martians, gilded pot metal; $100.
Courtesy of Skank World.

Glass Vases, designed by Thomas Stearns for Venini, Italy. Cylindrical vessels decorated with spiral threading above a gunmetal vase: left, unsigned but with paper label; 11⅛ inches high (didn't sell); center, inscribed VENINI/ITALIA. labeled MURANO; 14½ inches high (didn't sell); right, unsigned but with paper label; 9½ inches high; $2,875.

Courtesy of Sotheby's.

Glass Vase, designed by Toshi Iwata for Murano, c. 1968. Clear body, mold-blown with V decoration folded into hanky form with dense internal bubbles and internal amethyst bands; 5 inches high; $200.

Courtesy of John Toomey and Don Treadway, Toomey-Treadway Galleries, Oak Park, IL.

Vase, designed by Dale Chihuly. Part of his Macchia series, these used combinations of brilliant color and mottled exteriors, blown glass, ruffled edges. This one was done in the 1980s, but it is included as an example of his technique; $6,050.

Courtesy of Skinner Inc. Boston/Bolton, MA

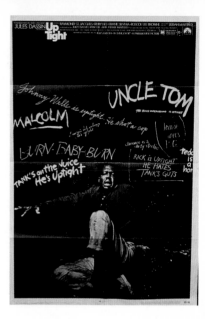

*P*oster, c.1968. Black protest movie poster, Up Tight; *27 x 41 inches; $45.*
Courtesy of John Kisch.

*C*enterfold, two-sided. Yellow Submarine, from Variety magazine promotional ad; *17 x 36 inches; $300.*
Courtesy of the author.

*P*oster, designed by Hans Emi, Swiss, c. 1973; *50 x 36 inches; $450.*
Courtesy of Poster Graphics.

Smiley items. Mugs and cookie jar; mugs, $25; cookie jar, $75.

Courtesy of Have a Nice Day Shop.

Sun Glasses and Envelope Purses. Designed by Peter Max. $200 each. *Courtesy of Larry Clemons Collection.*

Bellbottom Trousers, Beatles
Patch Pocket, c. 1970s. $350.
Courtesy of Have a Nice Day Shop.

Two Poncho Coats, both 1960s.
Wool, both with leather trim and
leather string belts: left, winter,
Bonnie Cashin style, $300; right,
fleece, Bonnie Cashin label, $400.
Courtesy of the author.

Dress, Paco Rabanne, c. 1968.
France, metallic link sheath; $750.
*Courtesy of Dykeman/Young,
Molly's Vintage Promotions.*

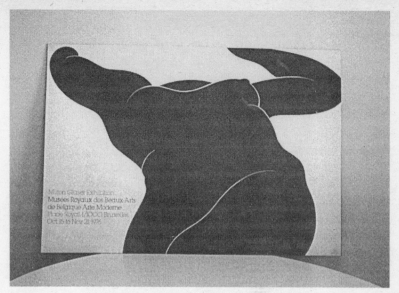

Poster, Milton Glazer Exhibition, c. 1976. Overscale nude for Musees Royauz de Beaux Arts de Belgique Arte Moderne; 2 feet × 3 feet; $900. Courtesy of Decor Moderne.

Collectors search for his psychedelic posters, which are still reasonably priced.

❋ ART POSTERS ❋

PRICES

New York State Theater—Lincoln Center, Robert Indiana, 1964. Early poster by famous "Love" artist; 30 inches × 45 inches; mint condition; $325.

Lot of Three Posters: First, *Autoportrait with "Love,"* Robert Indiana, c. 1980, unsigned, photolithograph on paper; second, American School, twentieth century, unsigned Op Art poster, silk screen in tones of gray on paper; third, *List Art Poster*, Richard Anusckiewicz, 1968, signed and dated "ANUSCK-

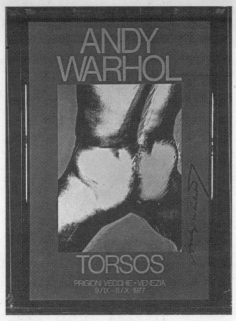

Poster, Torsos, *by Andy Warhol, c. 1977. For Prigioni Vecchie-Venezia, promotion for suite, hand-signed in black pen by Warhol, glazed and framed; 40 inches × 28 inches; $920.* Courtesy of Sotheby's Inc.

IEWICZ 1968" in pencil, annotated TO THE COLLECTION, green print on paper; sizes to 50½ inches × 50½ inches; $200/set.

Andy Warhol Signed *Torsos* Poster, for Prigioni Vecchie-Venezia, 9/IX-8/X, 1977. Promotion for suite; hand-signed in black pen by Warhol; glazed and framed; 40 inches × 28 inches; $920.

Andy Warhol Signed *The American Indian* Poster, for Ace Gallery, Canada, 1976. Promotion for *The American Indian Series* suite; hand-signed in black pen by Warhol; glazed and framed; 50 inches × 34 inches; $1,035.

PRICES

Minis to Motorcycles

Barbarella, Paramount, 1968. Jane Fonda, David Hem-

Poster, c. 1968. Barbarella movie advertisement; $150. Courtesy Modern Props.

mings, "See Barbarella Do Her Thing!"; full color; 27 inches ×
41 inches; mint condition; $150.

How to Stuff a Wild Bikini, American International, 1965.
Annette Funicello, Dwayne Hickman; full color; 27 inches × 41
inches; near-mint condition; $50.

Hey Let's Twist, Paramount, 1962. Joey Dee, The Starliters,
The Peppermint Loungers; shows the dancers; shows the place;
in red, black, and white; 27 inches × 41 inches; near-mint condition; $85.

Hell's Bloody Devils, Independent-International Pictures, c.
1964. John Gabriel, Broderick Crawford; "Madmen on Motor-
cycles"; 27 inches × 41 inches; near-mint condition; $65.

Muscle Beach Party, American International, 1964. Frankie
Avalon, Annette Funicello; full color; 27 inches × 41 inches;
near-mint condition; $75.

Miniskirt Mob, American International, 1968. Jeremy Slate, Diane McBaine; "Hog Straddling Female Animals on the Prowl"; photo montage in pink, purple, and gray; 27 inches × 41 inches; fine condition; $65.

Twist All Night, American International, 1962. Louis Prima, June Wilkinson; great 1960s' two-color design; 27 inches × 41 inches; near-mint condition; $100.

Protest Posters

Dickie Bird, c. 1969. Black-and-white lithograph; comic illustration of Nixon as motorcycle outlaw; well done; complete with protest buttons saying "I get high with a little help from my friends"; 22 inches × 30 inches; mint condition; $50.

Easy Rider, c. 1969. Classic 1960s movie image; Peter Fonda and Dennis Hopper riding choppers across desert; full color; blue border; 35 inches × 23 inches; mint condition; $60.

Family Plot, Champion Products, © 1971. Cartoonlike image of huge gravestone reading "America, the United States Of, Born 1776, Died 1980s After Swallowing a Fatal Dose of War and Pollution . . ."; done in black, white, and brown; 17 inches × 22 inches; mint condition; $50.

Father Time, International Poster Corporation, © 1968. Surreal imagery of Lyndon Johnson as the Grim Reaper seated atop shadowy, burnt-orange globe; no caption, certainly none is needed; great antiwar image; 21 inches × 30 inches; mint condition; $75.

For All Time, © Compass Points, c. 1970. Silk screened blacklight poster in vibrant greens, blues, black; classic Iwo Jima marines raising peace symbol flag; 22 inches × 34 inches; mint condition; $75.

Graffiti, c. 1968. Black-and-white blowup of interiors of men's room with all types of typical 1960s sayings on the wall; 20 inches × 30 inches; mint condition; $35.

Hitler Quote, c. 1969. "'The streets of our country are in turmoil, the universities are filled with students rebelling and rioting. . . . We need Law and Order!'—Adolph Hitler, 1932";

letters in white against glossy red background and graphic of upside-down flag; 19 inches × 26 inches; mint condition; $65.

In Peace Sons Bury Their Fathers . . . , Marquesette Litho, Chicago, © 1972. "'In War Fathers Bury Their Sons.'—Herodotus"; chilling antiwar image showing blowup of old photo of young boy seated on steps; searing rush of red, white, and blue blots at left; 23 inches × 35 inches; mint condition; $90.

Suppose They Gave a War and Nobody Came, c. 1968, Rich, hand-pulled silk screen blacklight typographic poster that highlights a number of the letters in the text to spell the word *peace* in red amid yellow letter forms; 22 inches × 30 inches; mint overall condition; $50.

The Great Society, International Poster Corporation, © 1968. Great Gustaf Dore-like image of Lyndon B. Johnson at the throne of the Angel of Death; done in blues, purples, and black; 21 inches × 28 inches; mint condition; $90.

This Vacation, Visit Beautiful Vietnam, c. 1970. "Fly Far-Fareastern Airways"; antiwar blacklight poster done in orange and black; no credits or copyright mark; battle scene at bottom; passenger jet streams across top in travel poster motif; 22 inches × 35 inches; mint condition; $75.

Vietnam Brisk Tea, c. 1968. Three-color lithograph; comic protest poster showing a man holding teacup in one hand and a lit roach in the other; labellike seal at the left says "Selected by VC/and Green Berets"; 23 inches × 27 inches; mint condition; $50.

Vietnamization, Western Graphics, Eraser's Edge, © 1970. Fabulous black-and-white image on heavy stock showing close image of dozens of clay sculptures of Richard M. Nixon in "coolie" hats, an absolute delight; certainly scarce; 28 inches × 22 inches; mint condition; $125.

Would You Die to Save This Face?, International Poster Corporation, © 1968. Stern Lyndon B. Johnson in engravinglike image in blue and black against red and white stripes; 21 inches × 29 inches; mint condition; $75.

Killed in Action—Stop, by Dunstan Periera, Universal

Poster Company, © 1970. Powerful photo montage of huge footprint in the sand—reminiscent of the Moon Landing footprint, one of the strong graphic images of the late 1960s—littered with spent cartridges; with ghostly image of mother and child and partially buried American banner; full color; 26 inches × 34 inches; mint condition; $65.

New Action Army, Speciality Imports, Memphis, Tennessee, c. 1968. Superrich blacklight silk screen image; dripping American flag with peace symbol at upper left rains down on soldier and Vietnamese prisoner amid large type reading "Our Flag, Our Future, Join the New Action Army"; 22 inches × 23 inches; mint condition; $65.

Peace, by Dean Eller, Kendrick and Associates, © 1970. Line of riot police holding nightsticks and facing line of hippies at top amid positive/negative design of swooping white dove in hyper red, white, and blue; 22 inches × 26 inches; mint condition; $90.

Peace Now, Emerson Graphics, San Francisco, © 1968. Photo lithograph done in blues; young boy walking in the rain under a peace sign–festooned umbrella; type at bottom reads "Mankind must put an end to war or war will put an end to mankind—John F. Kennedy"; 22 inches × 29 inches; mint condition; $45.

Phi Zappa Krappa, c. 1968. Vintage blowup of iconoclast Frank Zappa seated upon a commode; in black and white; 22½ inches × 29½ inches; mint condition; $45.

Pride Integrity Gallantry Service, c. 1969. Black-and-white photo posterization showing slovenly policeman with pig mask face; 23 inches × 35 inches; mint condition; $45.

Revolution, Guiniven, Specialty Imports, Memphis, Tennessee, c. 1968. Protest poster in black and white; dramatic image of U.S. soldier holding bayonet at throat of protester; type at top reads "In March 1770, a military unit took offense at being called names and pelted with rocks, fired into a group of unarmed civilians. They called it the Boston Massacre, then they started a revolution"; 18 inches × 23 inches; mint condition; $50.

Rise and Fall of the Fourth Reich, International Poster Corporation, c. 1968. Black and white; Lyndon B. Johnson drives a VW Beetle; done in the exact style of popular VW advertising of the 1906s; 21 inches × 30 inches; mint condition; $45.

Woodstock, Arno Skolinick, 1969. Aside from the well-known "I Want You" poster, this is the most famous of all American posters to the baby-boomer generation; white dove of peace; red background; 24 inches × 36 inches; $425.

Jewelry

Just as "anything goes" was the motto for clothing design in the 60s and 70s, so it was with jewelry. In fact, anything you decided to hang around your neck or wear on fingers, ears, arms, or toes was considered jewelry. However, there were designs made specifically with the Pop Art and hippie look of the times. Sometimes they came from recognized designers; sometimes amateurs tried their hand at it. The problem for collectors is to learn which is which. My advice is: if it's unusual, clearly defines the look of the era, and the price is cheap, buy now.

Everyone made jewelry; even the elegant fashion house of Hatti Carnegie made several lines of Pop Art jewelry in the late 1960s. Bill Smith hand-dyed acrylic and combined it with chrome in the late 50s and early 60s. Plastic became "art jewelry" in the hands of American designers Stanley Lechzin and Bob Natalini. Lechzin, a master jewelry designer, often com-

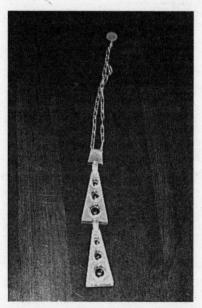

Necklace. Pop design metal necklace in form of collar and necktie with faux jewel tie-tacs, brass; $30. Courtesy of The Time Machine.

bined cast acrylics with previous metals and pearls. Artist and craftsman Natalini worked with cast polyester resin, also in combination with precious metals. Michael Mott jewelry used mirrored cubes and imbedded rhinestones.

With the advent of boutiques in the 1960s art jewelry found a niche, and trendy plastics often wore high price tags. Pieces by name artists were usually signed.

Many crafts jewelers turned to plastic because it could be so easily worked. Much of their jewelry can be found these days at thrift shops, or in vintage clothing shops, for just a few dollars.

At top couture salons such as Ungaro famous sculptors were often commissioned to design jewelry. Among them was Giso Pomodoro, who created necklaces and pendants.

FRIEDRICH BECKER (1922–   )

This German jewelry designer gained prominence in the 60s with his avant-garde, kinetic jewelry. Educated at the Werk-kunstschule in Dusseldorf, he graduated in 1951. In 1952, he earned a master's degree and opened his own workshop. Initially he was trained as a mechanical fitter in Dusseldorf, prior to his apprenticeship as a goldsmith and silversmith.

By the 60s his designs had become minimalist and geometric, focusing on movement and variability. Using precious metals and gemstones, he created wearable kinetic art. He used metal rods joined by articulated axles with spring pressure to create pieces that could assume different positions. Invisible micro ball bearings allowed disks, bars, and cones with balanced weights to rotate and move in opposite directions—at various angles and speeds. The wearer and gravity caused the designs to move. His necklaces were prime examples of the creative current of the times; he created art with industrial forms.

He retired in 1982 from his position as a professor at the Fackhochscule in Dusseldorf, but still designs jewelry today.

Irena Brynner (1917–   )

Though this Russian artist became well known during the late 1950s for her sculptural and organic-style jewelry, her kinetic jewelry of the 1960s was an instant success. Her work, mostly in gold, focused on using the lost-wax technique with centrifugal casting. It allowed her to create rings with twisted and rolled edges that seemed to be sculpted, often in vegetal shapes. She combined gold with novel stones. To date her work hasn't turned up at auction, giving collectors a chance to hunt it down for reasonable prices. Note that her initials ("IB" in a circle) are impressed on the inside of her rings.

Sam Kramer (1913–1964)

Always avant-garde, Kramer proved that almost any material could be incorporated into jewelry. His parents moved to Southern California during the Depression and Kramer graduated from the University of Southern California in 1936. He took a jewelry course there, and shortly after graduation returned to his native Pittsburgh, where he worked for a jewelry manufacturer. He developed an interest in Navaho jewelry, and after spending a couple of years in Pittsburgh with his wife, Carol, they moved to New York. In 1939 he studied gemology at New York University, and he subsequently opened a shop on Eighth Avenue.

Unlike the makers of much Modern design jewelry, Kramer avoided geometric forms. Instead his pieces hinted at Surrealism, whether with a red taxidermy glass eye on a sterling silver cuff bracelet or with his use of semiprecious stones. His glass eyes became something of a trademark. However, in all of his jewelry, the joke seems to be on the eye of the beholder.

Today, even though he is widely considered one of the most innovative and influential American jewelry designers of the Modern movement, his pieces are priced on the low side when they come to auction. He continued working until his death in 1964, developing new forms that fit in with radical 60s fashions.

PRICES

Amber Bracelets, 18K yellow gold, number 6 of 25, Amalia Del Ponte, 1969. Made by Gem Montebello, Milan; $8,800.

Sculptured Ring, 18K yellow gold, number 12 of 20, Guitou Knoop. Made by Emil Schaffner, marked "GK"; $880.

18K Gold and Enamel Pin/Pendants, 1974. Leaping nanna in blue body with pink, black, and white corsette with detachable male figure; signed "NIKI DE SAINT PHALLE"; number 1 of a series of 3, manufactured by Gem Montebello; $6,875.

18K Yellow and White Gold Ring, 1968. Movable filaments and lapis lazuli; number 9 of 20; signed "JESUS RAPHAEL SOTO" and dated "68"; manufactured by Gem Montebello; $2,200.

Georg Jensen Silver Arm Ring, designed by Thor Selzer, introduced in 1972. Cast and open sterling; stamped "GEORG JENSEN 236 I.D."; 2¼ inches wide; $200.

Sterling Silver Necklace, 1977. Matte-finished, geometric design; suspended from an elongated chain; hallmarked "Finland"; $132.

18K Yellow Gold Bracelet, Guitou Knoop. "Day Moon"; number 2 of 8; marked "EMIL SCHAFFNER"; 46.2 pennyweight; $132.

18K Yellow Gold, Diamond, and Sapphire Bracelet, c. 1960. Reeded grid pattern links alternating with eighteen diamonds; approximate total weight of diamonds 1.10 carats; 18 sapphires, approximate total weight 1.30 carats; 35.5 pennyweight; 6¾ inches long; $1,320.

18K Yellow Gold Ring, Pol Bury, 1972. Kinetic; number 16 of 30; with moving spheres, hallmarked "Gem Montebello, Milan"; $1,650.

18K Gold Shell Pin, Kurt Wayne, 1971. Designed as a conch shell; 14.0 pennyweight; $770.

18K Bicolor Gold Band, Dinhvan for Cartier, c. 1970. Alternating yellow and white coils; 10.7 pennyweight; $715.

14K/18K Yellow Gold Lion Pendant and 14K Gold Chain, c. 1970. Large stylized lion; highlighted by round diamonds, sapphires, emeralds, and rubies within a textured frame; with matching heavy link chain; 110.2 pennyweight; $990.

YVES SAINT LAURENT

Yves Saint Laurent designed costume jewelry, examples of which are beginning to find their way to vintage clothing auctions.

PRICES

Yves Saint Laurent Star Brooch, 1960s. Gold metal wire with Baroque faux pearls; marked "YSL"; $40–$60.

Yves Saint Laurent Necklace, 1960s. Silver and gold tone tube beads with spherical bead; marked "YSL"; $75–$100.

Yves Saint Laurent Sautoir a Pastilles, 1960s. Gilt frame glass and beads in purple, green, and brick red; marked "YSL"; $200–$300.

Pair of Yves Saint Laurent Bright Aquamarine Rhinestone Earrings, 1960s. Marked "YSL," together with a pair of black square earrings set with rhinestones; $75–100/set.

KENNETH JAY LANE

Kenneth Jay Lane's costume jewelry became popular in the mid-1960s, first with wealthy avant-garde New Yorkers, who also espoused anything done by Pop artist and filmmaker Andy Warhol. Lane's jewelry is currently among the most popular with collectors. His pieces later sold in the jewelry departments of such stores as I. Magnin and were worn by men as well. In fact, men wore both American and East Indian jewelry, along with shell necklaces from the South Pacific.

PRICES

Kenneth Jay Lane Earrings (pair), 1960. Ruby faceted beads set in pewter metal; marked "KJL"; $115.

Ed Wiener (1918–1991)

Wiener was self-taught; his only formal training as a jewelry maker came in 1945, when he enrolled in a general craft course at Columbia University. He was intrigued by the neoprimitive shapes being exhibited at that time by Alexander Calder. Shortly afterward he began working out of his home, creating monogram pins from silver wire. In 1946, he and his wife opened a studio, where he sold his own designs along with Mexican jewelry. In 1947 he opened a store, Arts and Ends, and in 1953 he opened a second store in Greenwich Village. One of his most important pieces, titled "The Dancer," was inspired by a 1941 photo of dancer Martha Graham. It is cut from sheet silver into a biomorphic shape that defines the dancer's body. One hundred copies were made. His signature, "Ed Wiener," is usually impressed on his work.

Examples of his work from the mid-60s through the 70s

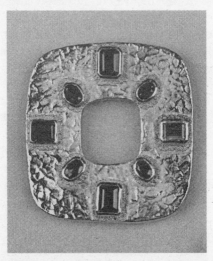

Brooch, signed Ed Wiener, c. 1970. Multi-stone, 18k yellow gold hammered square collect-set with various color tourmalines with beaded accents; 34.9 dwt; $1,800–2,200. Courtesy of Skinner Inc., Boston/Bolton, MA.

showed the influence of trips to the medieval Museé de Cluny in Paris and to gem-cutting centers in Jaipur, India. Much of his jewelry from this period had a Byzantine look, incorporating textured gold and stones. He continued working until his recent death.

TORUN (VIVIANNA) BULOW-HUBE (1927–   )

One of the most important Scandinavian silversmiths, Swedish Vivianna Bulow-Hube is equally at home designing glass, jewelry, and ceramics. Over the years she has designed for Georg Jensen Silversmithy, Cristofle, Orrefors, and Dansk International. Educated at the State School of Arts, Crafts and Design in her native Sweden, she began working in Stockholm in 1948. Her early jewelry designs of the 1950s relied on simple design and the use of such ordinary materials as glass and pebbles combined with silver. By the late 1960s her designs had become sculptural, from a mobile-form necklace to a coffee service.

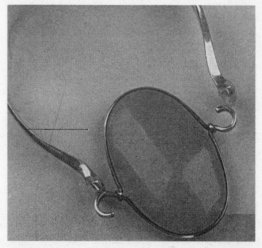

Cuff Bracelet, signed Georg Jensen, designed by Torun-Bulow-Hube, c. 1960s. Sterling silver and rutilated quartz, with large oval quartz; $300–400. Courtesy of Skinner Inc., Boston/Bolton, MA.

Noteworthy examples include:

- Coffee service for Georg Jensen, c. 1960.
- Silver coffer-boxes, c. 1963.
- Wristwatches in stainless steel with sculptural form; for Georg Jensen, c. 1969.

❀ OTHER JEWELRY DESIGNS ❀

Bar Brooch, c. 1960. Green, topaz, and clear rhinestones; marked "DEPOSE"; $92.

Choker, 1960s. With fringes of faceted amber, black, and crystal beads; $57.

Choker Necklace, 1960s. Flat, round, gilt metal links and rhinestone spheres; $172.

Czechoslovakian Choker, c. 1969. Set with rhinestone buckle; beaded fringe and ruby velvet band; $57.

Domed Brooch, 1960s. Faux coral cabochons, canary rhinestones, and swirly coral glass cabochons; $80.

Flower Brooch, 1960s. Gold and silver gilt metal loops with faux topaz center; marked "DEPOSE"; $345.

Four-Strand Necklace. Purple, forest green, ruby, or amber lozenge glass beads with gold scalloped caps; with a matching pendant on a gilt metal wire choker; $316/set.

Fringed Rhinestone Choker, 1960s. Flexibly set in gilt metal with smoky marquise rhinestones and faceted beads; $201.

Gold Rhinestone Cluster Clip, 1960s. Marked "DEPOSE"; $103.

Gripoix Brooch, 1970s. Black glass shooting stars; marked "FRANCE"; $575.

Pair of Gripoix-Style Chandelier Earrings, 1960s. Flexible chain links set with yellow, aqua, blue, lavender, and rose cabochons and rhinestones; marked "FRANCE"; $517.

Indian Choker, 1960s. Set with faux turquoise stones and bells; $69.

Indian Choker, 1960s. Mirror-enameled and pendants strung on red cord; some losses; $57.

Indian Pendant, 1960s. White metal and coral beads on a chain; $23.

Indian Festoon Necklace, 1960s. Mirror-enameled; faux pearls and faux turquoise small beads; $115.

Indian Choker, 1960s. White metal ornamented with tiny bells; $57.

Two Indian Plaque Brooches, 1960s. Gilt filigree set with faceted faux agate and amber beads; $46/set.

Indian Foil-Backed Glass Set Pendant, 1960s. On a chain; $11.

Pair of Indian Mirror-Enameled Chandelier Earrings, 1960s. $46.

Pair of Indian Mirror-Enameled Chandelier Earrings, 1960s. $46.

Pair of Indian Chandelier Earrings, 1960s. With turquoise enamel and faux pearls; $17.

Indian Beaded Necklace, 1960s. Amber, blue, and faux pearl beads with fringes; $28.

Jewel-Studded Disk Pendant, 1960s. On a gilt metal snake chain; $34.

Jomaz Starburst Brooch, 1960s. Faux turquoise and lapis cabochons and rhinestones; marked "JOMAZ"; $258.

Multistrand Necklace, 1960s. Miniscule gilt metal beads; faux pearls of various shapes and sizes joined by gilt metal chain links; $287.

Necklace, 1960s. Silver tone snake and other chain links with numerous gold metal and silver metal pendants; $80.

Oversize Bead Necklace, 1960s. In gilt metal with large disk spacers at intervals; $172.

Sandor Company Choker, c. 1969. Golden mesh with chain fringe below black enameled plaque; $103.

Sautoir A. Pastilles, 1960s. Gilt-framed faceted stones and faceted beads in pale blue, amber, red purple, and green; $172.

Starburst Brooch, 1960s. Stiff chain links; $80.

Two Necklaces, 1960s. The first a choker of graduated clear plastic beads with hammered gilt metal pendants; the second of pierced and carved bone beads with silver metal tips; $143/set.

Triangular Bib Necklace, 1960s. Silver and gold tone flying saucer disks; $34.

Necklaces with Pendants (three), 1960s. Long snake chain with a hammered gilt metal pendant, set with blue and green cabochon stones; gold and silver flower power medallion on a long chain; and chain with pendant, both studded with amber and pewter cabochons, the pendant marked "PARIS"; $143/set.

Pendant Necklaces (three), 1960s. Comprising a gold fluted, faux seed pearl and lapis bead necklace with five lapis African face medallions; gilt metal fluted bead, Baroque faux pearl, and turquoise plastic barbell bead necklace with turquoise plastic Chinese gourd pendant; and gilt metal fluted bead, crystal rock, and hammered bead necklace with carved ram's head ornament; $103/set.

Triple Strand Necklace, 1960s. Of gilt metal beads studded with crystal dangles; $920.

Two Necklaces and a Choker, 1960s. Two bright gilt metal chain link encrusted fluted white plastic bead necklaces; gilt metal tipped large faux pearl choker with silver disk spacers; $34/set.

Vogue Paisley Pendant, 1960s. Set with red and green stones on a long golden chain; marked "VOGUE"; $80.

Lighting

Shop Light, c. 1960. Oversized light bulb with metal cage; $145. Courtesy of Modern Times.

In these two decades lighting design took on a sculptural aspect that continued the organic look of the fifties and added trendy Pop elements. Plastic was the material of choice, especially with such Italian designers as Joe Colombo, the Castiglioni brothers, Gae Aulenti, and Mario Bellini. Some were made of PVC pipe and were multidirectional. Others used acrylics to create fanciful, often complex, shapes that were in effect sculptural. The light weight of the plastic allowed designers to work in large scale. But most important, it was the diffusing characteristics, which differed in the wide selection of plastics available, that gave lighting its distinctive 60s beauty. Among the most popular plastics for this purpose were glossy ABS and acrylic.

A good example of an acrylic design of the period is the Columbo table lamp of 1962. Acrylic and shaped as a wave, it used only a small fluorescent bulb. Lighting was minimal, but the sculptural effect was dramatic.

AKARI ASSOCIATES
This subsidiary of the Isamu Noguchi Foundation has managed and coordinated worldwide sales of a line of electric lamps

*Table Lamp, c. 1968. Lucite and molded styrene; 6 inches high × 6
inches deep × 28 inches wide; $100.* Courtesy of Fat Chance.

*Medusa Lamp, late 1960s. Aluminum tubing and chrome, five tentacles;
52 inches high; $300.* Courtesy of Anthony Du Pont Collection.

known as Akari from 1951 to the present. These lamps are all
based on designs of sculptor Isamu Noguchi. They are manufactured in Gifu, Japan, by Ozeki and Company, Ltd. The first
Akari lamps were small-scale table models. In 1961, standing
lamps were made with fluorescent tubes. Because so many
cheap copies were made by others, in 1969 Noguchi created
signed limited editions of thirty new designs.

More than sixty Akari styles are being made, from the earliest examples to the current line of pyramidal modules. Though
the following pieces date from the 1980s, they provide examples of the style and price range for collectible Akari.

PRICES

Isamu Noguchi Floor Lamp, manufactured by Akari, c.
1980. Ovaloid paper-and-bamboo shade supported by three-

legged wire rod base; 48 inches high × 18 inches in diameter; excellent condition; $329.

Isamu Noguchi Hanging Fixture, manufactured by Akari, c. 1982. Staggered triangular form of wire and paper that creates a six-pointed star configuration; 49 inches high × 11 inches deep × 11 inches wide; excellent condition; $230.

Isamu Noguchi Wall Sconce, manufactured by Akari, c. 1980. Ovaloid form with off-center cutout to create biomorphic image; 9 inches high × 19 inches deep × 20 inches wide; excellent condition; $170.

ACHILLE CASTIGLIONI (1918–   )

One of Italy's most renowned postwar architects and exhibition and industrial designers, Achille Castiglioni studied architecture at the Politecnico in Milan. He began his career as a free-lance designer in Milan in 1944, working with his brothers Livio Castiglioni (1944–1945) and Pier Giacomo Castiglioni (1944–1968). He designed for Alessi, Arteluce, Ideal Standard, Kartell, Knoll, and others. His work is in permanent collections at the Museum of Modern Art, New York; the Victoria and Albert Museum, London, and the Staatliches Museum fur Angewandte Kunst, Munich. Among his most important works are:

- The Tubino lamp, c. 1951, produced by Flos, then reproduced in 1974.

- Mezzadro stool in steel, 1957, for Zanotta, reproduced in 1971.

- Lierna chair, first produced in 1960 by Gavina, and again in 1969 by Knoll International.

- Arco lamp, produced by Flos, 1962.

- Leonardo work desk with glass or plastic laminate top, for Zanotta, 1968.

- Parentesi floor-to-ceiling suspension lamp, for Flos in 1971.

Pier Giacomo Castiglioni (1913–1968)

This Italian architect and exhibition, interior, and industrial designer did much of his work with his brothers Achille and Livio. He studied architecture at the Politecnico in Milan. He designed for Arteluce, Kartell, Krupp, Zanotta, and others. His work is in collections at the Victoria and Albert Museum, London; the Museum of Modern Art, New York; and others. Among his best-known designs are:

- Cavalletto table, produced in 1955 by Gavina.
- KD51/Teli lamp, produced by Kartell, 1959, and by Flos in 1973.
- Arco lamp, produced by Gavina, 1962.
- Relemme pendant lamp, produced by Flos, 1962.
- Snoopy table lamp, produced by Flos in 1967.

PRICES

Livio Castiglioni and Gianfranco Frattini Hoover-Pipe-Shape Plastic Lamp Boalum, produced by Artemide, c. 1970. Elongated swirled cream spring coated with transparent plastic; enclosing a succession of light bulbs; impressed ARTEMIDE MADE IN ITALY; MODELLO BOALUM DESIGN: LIVIO CASTIGLIONI GIANFRANCO FRATTINI; 75 inches long; $1,150.

❈ OTHER LIGHTING DESIGNS ❈

Vico Magistretti/Artemide, Milan, Giunone (Juno) Floor Lamp, c. 1969. Enameled metal; a variation of his famous eclipse table lamp with rotating spherical metal shades; 90 inches high × 26 inches deep × 26 inches wide; excellent condition; $500.

Gae Aulenti/Artemide Pileino Lamp, c. 1972. Adjustable lamp of molded plastic construction with chromium-plated steel; metal fittings; white enameled steel base; original finish; 55 inches high × 16 inches in diameter; excellent condition; $450.

Italian Floor Lamp, c. 1960s. Op Art barbell form of yellow

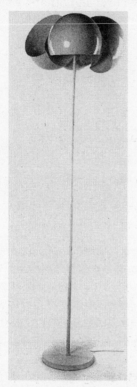 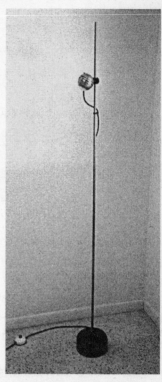

Juno Floor Lamp, designed by Vico Magistretti, manufactured by Artemide, Milan, Italy, c. 1969. Enameled metal, a variation of his famous eclipse table lamp showing another possibility of movement with four rotating, spherical metal shades; 90 inches high × 26 inches deep × 26 inches wide; $500. Courtesy of Treadway Gallery.

Floor Lamp, Italy. Stainless steel with cast-iron base, paper label: ARREDOULCE MONZA; 63 inches high; $1,500. Courtesy of Decor Moderne.

Arteluce Table Lamp, c. 1960s. High-tech design with a square transformer base; 26 inches high × 6 inches in diameter; $120.

Modern Chrome Arc Floor Lamp, after Achille and Pier Giacomo Castiglioni Arco Design, c. 1970. Iron base with adjustable aluminum dome hood; 72 inches high; $192.50.

and white enameled steel that pivots on circular Lucite base, rewired; 56 inches high × 7 inches in diameter; excellent condition; $280.

Arteluce Table Lamp, c. 1960s. Extremely sophisticated high-tech design with a square transformer base; enamel shaft with pop-out vented spotlight and a brushed aluminum shade that revolves on a highly polished chrome ball; very rare and unusual; base 26 inches high × 6 inches in diameter; excellent condition; $120.

Modern Chrome Arc Floor Lamp, after Achille and Pier Giacomo Castiglioni Arco Design, c. 1970. Iron base with tele-

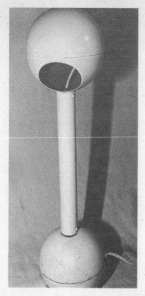

Floor Lamp, Italian, c. 1960s. Op Art barbell form of white enameled steel that pivots on circular lucite base; 21 inches high × 5 inches in diameter; $280. Courtesy of Toomey-Treadway Galleries, Oak Park, IL.

Table Lamp, Murano, c. 1960s. Colorless glass pedestal base with circular white, floating shade; 21 inches high × 12 in diameter; $110. Courtesy of Toomey-Treadway Galleries, Oak Park, IL.

scopic steel arc and adjustable aluminum dome hood; unsigned; 72 inches high with 6-inch radius; $192.50.

Gino Sarfatti Wand Lamp, made by Arteluce, c. 1960. Conical weighted black base supporting thin tubular chrome pole with adjustable cylindrical shades; 76 inches high × 2 inches deep × 10 inches wide; excellent condition; $350.

Chrome Floor Lamp, c. 1970. Interlocking squares and rectangles set on painted wood base; 62½ inches high × 9 inches deep × 9 inches wide; $50.

Fontana Art Glass and Stainless Steel Lamp, designed by Gio Ponti, c. 1968. Lozenge section fixture in grid-patterned frosted glass with stainless steel mounts; unsigned; 14¾ inches high; $3,162.

Table Lamp, Italian, c. late 1960s. Dark metal made with blow torch, signed FANTONI; *24 inches high × 9 inches wide; $1,200.* Courtesy of Decor Moderne.

Saffo Table Lamp, designed by Archimede Seguso, c. 1967. Smoked and white glass and polished metal; 13 inches high; $450. Courtesy of Anthony Du Pont Collection.

Lamp, c. 1960s. Shade of half circle within a larger half circle, both of which rotate to adjust light; chrome shaft circular base; red enamel; 18 inches high × 10 inches in diameter; mint condition; $300.

Three Glass Hurricane Shade, c. 1960. Each double-waisted cylindrical vessel in clear glass; decorated with red, blue, and green canes in a spiral pattern; 10¼ inches high; $690.

Venini Ceiling Fixture, c. 1960. Oversized globe form of transparent white glass with irregular dramatic orange band of rolled glass; original chrome fitting; 18 inches in diameter; mint condition; $160.

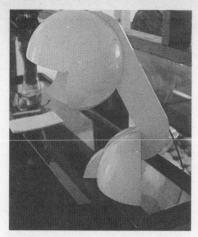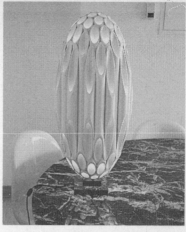

The Ruspa Table Lamp, designed by Gae Allendi, Italian, manufactured by Martinelli, c. 1968. White enameled metal, adjustable; 22 inches high × 13 inches wide; $2,400. Courtesy of Al Eiber Collection.

Lamp, designed by Rougier, c. 1969. PVC plastic mounted on black marble base, used as the "brain" on a "Star Trek" episode; 31 inches high × 13 inches wide; $400. Courtesy of Anthony Du Pont Collection.

Miscellaneous

Since the 1970s serious collectors have been concentrating on what has come to be lumped under the umbrella of "collectibles." This has included give-aways, limited-edition objects, sports memorabilia and advertising items, to mention just a few. More recently this covers 1960s and 1970s football cards, a variety of TV-related subjects from TV personality dolls and toys to TV guides, and original TV guide illustrations. Always popular Militaria now includes the Korean and Vietnam Wars. Space subjects that are sought included everything from cookie jars to TV show material. However, inasmuch as this book is mostly concerned with historical and sociological influences as they related to designs, it has narrowed down the categories rather brief mentions just to give you tips on potential new collectibles.

❀ INDUSTRIAL DESIGNS ❀

TV sets were designed in the 1960s by Maro Zanuso and Roger Tallon. Braun made an electric shaver (SM3, 1960), and companies like Braun, Phillips, and Moulinex designed such small kitchen appliances as coffee grinders, mixers, and juicers in the 60s. Holders for crayons and pens were designed by Georges Patrix and plastic table services were designed by Roger Tallon.

Even desk calendars were designed in plastic with the look of the mid to late 60s by Enzo Mari.

PRICES

JVC Television, c. 1972. Plastic shell in the form of a space helmet; 13 inches high; $50.

AT&T Experimental Phone, c. 1960s. Red base with clear bulbous form supporting rotary dial; perfect working order; $230.

Lucite Telephone, c. 1960s. Tubular clear phone with inte-

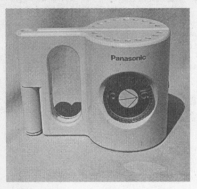

Coffee Maker, c. 1960s. Plastic, manufactured by Panasonic; $125; Courtesy of Fat Chance.

Radio and 8-track, c. 1970s. Plastic, space helmet, manufactured by Panasonic; $75. Courtesy of Anthony Du Pont Collection.

rior mechanisms visible; handset black and silver tone plastic; handset marked "ITT"; 10 inches in diameter × 18 inches high; very good condition; $155.

Jefferson Integer Cordless Electric Clock. Bulbous sculptural form of chrome-plated metal with angular face in gold with stripe decoration; stylized hands; 5 inches in diameter × 6 inches high; excellent condition; $20.

❀ KENNEDY COLLECTIBLES ❀

There's still plenty of magic associated with the Kennedy name—especially when it comes to presidential collectibles. There's nothing unusual about collecting presidential memorabilia, and currently the most popular items are those associated with President J. F. Kennedy. Generally they are divided into several categories, often overlapping into spin-offs such as toys and decorative accessories. Objects relating to the 1960 campaign appeal to political collectors. This specialized category

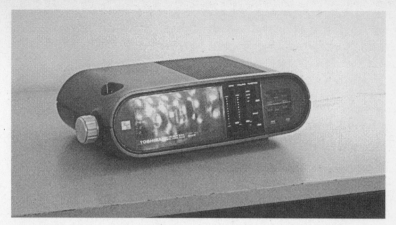

Clock Radio (AM/FM), late 1960s through 1970s. Solid state digital, manufactured by Toshiba, red, reinforced polyester plastic; $125. Courtesy of Anthony Du Pont Collection.

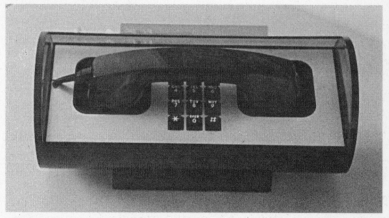

Early Digital Phone, c. 1972. Black plastic cover, AT&T; $75. Courtesy of Anthony Du Pont Collection.

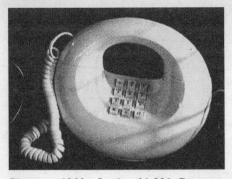

Phone, c. 1960s. Lucite; $1,001. Courtesy of HG Limited.

Table Clocks, c. 1965. Plastic, manufactured by Panasonic; each measures 5 × 3 inches; $25/each. Courtesy of Fat Chance.

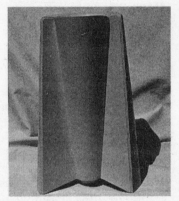

Polaroid Land Camera, SX-70, c. 1973. Light-brown vinyl with chrome trim, with case; $250. Courtesy Harvey Hesse Collection.

Vase, designed by Enzo Mari, Italy, c. 1969. Molded yellow plastic; 5 × 10 inches; $200. Courtesy of Fat Chance.

is covered in other books. Prices listed here are objects created during his popular administration and after his assassination. Included in the latter are JFK mourning buttons, still banks, comic books, and drinking glasses. Objects, such as the rocking chair, that came to be known as JFK symbols were used in a variety of ways.

Wall Hanging/Rug. Cotton velour, depicts President John F. Kennedy; 36 × 20 inches; $200. Courtesy of Modern Props.

PRICES

John F. Kennedy and His Rocking Chair Japanese Tin Toy, by Kamar, 1964. Original box, tags, newspaper; music box; $200–$400.

❋ PLAYBOY COLLECTIBLES ❋

The Playboy Enterprises were certainly one of the important influences in the 60s sexual revolution, and they created a myriad of collectibles. The promotion-minded company that began with Hugh Hefner's launching of *Playboy* magazine in 1953 expanded into clubs, casinos, and merchandise. When it all ended in the 1970s it left behind a new category for collectors.

In 1953 Arthur Paul, an American exhibition and graphic designer, was hired by Hefner to design the Playboy Bunny logo. Prior to that commission he was considered an important influence on the illustration liberation movement, and was the winner of many design awards, but he is best remembered for his work with Playboy Enterprises.

Collectors have a chance to get in on the ground floor, since most of these items can be found cheaply at garage sales and flea markets. Exceptions are first editions of the magazine, which can sell from the high hundreds to over a thousand dollars. Since this is a specialized field, collectors should check for sources (listed in the back of this book). In the case of paper items, collectors should look for pieces in mint condition.

PRICES

Mug. Plastic; black with white Playboy logo; $10.

Paperweight. Glass with etched Playboy logo; promotional giveaway; $30.

❃ PROTEST COLLECTIBLES ❃

Items made to protest the various social problems, women's liberation, and the Vietnam War, for example, could very well be the next "hot" collectibles category. To give you a brief idea of what to look for, some possibilities are listed below. A collection can be assembled based on either the entire protest atmosphere of the 60s and 70s or more specialized categories. As always, condition and rarity are most important things to consider when you're looking to buy.

THE CIVIL RIGHTS MOVEMENT

The 1963 civil rights March on Washington resulted not only in the beginning of Rev. Martin Luther King Jr.'s dream but

---

Buttons. Martin Luther King and Black Rights, March on Washington, 1963; $150. Courtesy of Harvey Hesse Collection.

also engendered a wealth of civil rights songs and collectibles. There were banners, billboards, posters, hand-carried signs, and buttons—to say nothing of the newspaper headlines from around the country. While many were trashed after the march, a few are coming to light, mostly at garage sales and flea markets. Prices depend on where you find a particular item.

PEACE SYMBOLS
From T-shirts to jewelry and lamp shades, the peace and love signs left some memorable collectibles behind. Wastebaskets, lamp shades, and wall hangings all serve as a reminder of the Vietnam War.

Love and Peace Symbols: Peace sticker, $3; sterling silver pin with LOVE, $50; Peach patch, flag motif, $10/each. Courtesy of Have a Nice Day.

Men's Belts (pair): American Indian with psychedelic enamel-bead design, $150; Leather belt with brass buckle and peace sign, manufactured by Ord Latgo, c. 1960s, $50. Courtesy of Anthony Du Pont Collection.

Book, Steal This Book, by Abbe Hoffman, c. 1971, Pirate Editions, New York; $40. Courtesy of Doug Gilbert.

* * *

Psychedelic

* * * * *

There were many sources that inspired and brought about the popularity of psychedelic art in the 60s. Like other art movements, it was clearly influenced by the late-nineteenth-century graphics of Alphonse Mucha and Toulouse-Lautrec. The use of strong, directly opposing colors placed side by side, often combined with swirling colors, had its roots in the 1930s and 1940s. There is nothing new about Op Art, either. Compare it with the motifs of tribal cultures such as tribal Oriental rugs and American Indian designs as well as early woven coverlets.

The field for collectors depends generally on good luck, since as of this writing many dealers are out hunting for pieces themselves. As in any other collecting field, unless you plan on furnishing your home with the "complete" look, concentrating your energy on a particular category is the best approach. There are the general categories of clothing and furniture, with any number of spin-offs that include Peter Max designs and music festival and musical group memorabilia. Jewelry spin-offs include peace and protest symbols. For poster collectors, a specialty could be a combination of politics, peace, and protests. Even the innocuous "smilies" that began appearing on everything from pins to pitchers are being collected. But then, what isn't?

❋ PSYCHEDELIC POSTERS ❋

PRICES

"Garden of Eden," Hip Products Inc., Chicago, Illinois. Blacklight poster in a range of colors; 22 inches × 35 inches; $45.

"The Print Mint," San Francisco, California, c. 1966. Pink, white, and maroon; 15½ inches × 20⅜ inches; $250.

Jimi Hendrix Memorial Poster, Hip Products, Chicago, Illinois, c. 1970. Blacklight poster; Edward Phelps, Jr., artist; black, orange, purple, and blue; 22⅝ inches × 30 inches; $150.

Bob Dylan Poster. Milton Glazer, artist; blue, green, white, brown, pink, and orange; 21⅛ inches × 32⅛ inches; $200.

Satan's Encounter, 1973. Flocked; $8.

Easy Rider. $50.

Jimi Hendricks. $100.

Rip Van Winkle. $9.

Eight Fine Examples of 1960s Psychedelic Posters. Comprising Bill Graham Presents Quicksilver; Otis Redding; Bill Graham Presents "Batman"; Independence Ball '66; Sin Dance; Howlin' Wolf at the Avalon; The Golden Road to Unlimited Devotion; and "LOVE"; offered in hard spiral binder; all eight posters clean, sharp corners and edges; mint condition; $1,495.

Woodstock Memorabilia, 1969. Includes two posters from the most famous concert of all time, a Woodstock puzzle, original clip earrings, two tickets, a program, and a Woodstock robe covered in an all-over photographic image of the massive crowd; $3,105.

Large Collection of Family Dog and Bill Graham Posters. Seventy-two posters designed by artists such as Mouse, Kelly, Griffin, etc.; bands include Quicksilver, Big Brother and the Holding Company, Jefferson Airplane, Buffalo Springfield, Grateful Dead, Martha and the Vandellas, the Charlatans, Captain Beefhart, Howling Wolf, and many more; fifty-four of the posters are covered and mounted in a large, hard spiral binder; eighteen are loose (binder is included in the lot); $3,737.

Miscellaneous Group of Rock and Roll Posters, 1960s. Thirty-five posters by artists like Wes Wilson, Rick Griffin, Mouse; photos by Herb Greene; includes groups and events such as Blues Project, the Charlatans' Triptych, Velvet Underground, Big Brother and the Holding Company, Grateful Dead, Jefferson Airplane, New Year's Bash 1966 at the Filmore West, the Doors, Cream, and many more; all posters placed in a large hard-bound spiral binder (the binder is included in the lot); $3,450.

PRICES

Chair, manufactured by Reese, Stein and Company, Inc., c. 1970. Inflatable plastic; black and white psychedelic swirl design; made in Taiwan; 36 inches wide; $300.

Clock, manufactured by Westclox, c. 1979. Peace symbol face; blue, green, white, and yellow; 6½ inches in diameter; $125.

Clock, manufactured by Westclox. Peace sign motif; known as Peace Time; blue, green, white, and yellow; 6½ inches; $70.

Beaded Curtain, c. 1969. Plastic; brown, yellow, and orange; 60 inches long × 36 inches wide per section; $80.

Floor Pillows. Purple, orange, and blue-green psychedelic motif; 22 inches square; $50/each.

Footstool. Vinyl-covered cardboard box; dice motif; black and white; 14¼ inches × 14¼ inches × 12½ inches; $125.

Trinket Box, c. 1970. Wood with psychedelic decoupage overall, made by Jean Kirkland; $250. Courtesy of The Time Machine.

Mobile, Mr. Mitty's Mobiles, Santa Monica, California, c. 1970. Cardboard; fluorescent pink, orange, yellow, and black; 16 inches high; $50.

Paperweight. Pottery; letters on the sides form the word *Love;* $15.

Mexican Wall Hanger (God's Eye). Yarn wrapped over wood stick frame; various bright colors; 19 inches; $12.

Rock and Roll Memorabilia

For rock and roll collectors, the 1981 Sotheby's London auction, the first of its kind, kicked off this new category. In the United States, it was the 1984 New York Sotheby's Carousel Auction that started Americans on a collecting binge that just keeps getting bigger and bigger. It seems hard to believe, but back then, bidders thought it a bit outrageous when five unused tickets to a 1968 Beatles concert sold for $300. At the same auction, a Wurlitzer-style jukebox used by John Lennon in his apartment at the Dakota had a preauction estimate of $9,000. It found a buyer for $20,350. Never mind that this was simply a fancy jukebox with colored lights and bubble tubes. The fact that Lennon had used it in a room he called his "Club" put it over the top.

But 1988 was the undisputed "year of the celebrity auction." It was a field day for collectors of rock and roll items. All they needed was money and plenty of it. At that time the Elton John collection went to the Sotheby's London block and far surpassed estimates. What's more, it was private collectors doing the buying. One of the items, the "Stars and Stripes" spectacles, sold to a collector for $3,740. John's "Yellow Brick Road" suit sold to another collector for $8,976. The suit, from the early 70s, came with a shirt embroidered with song titles from the album. At the time, Sotheby's noted that the sale was interesting for the fact that new buyers and private collectors brought in winning bids. Back in June of that year, memorabilia donated by Michael Jackson, Madonna, and other music celebrities in rock and roll for a Sotheby's Collectors' Carousel Auction did just as well.

Two early collectors, Londoners Isaac Tigrett and Peter Morton, opened their famous Hard Rock Cafe in 1971 and used just a couple of pieces in the restaurant. It wasn't until 1984 that they used some of their rock and roll collection to decorate their New York Hard Rock Cafe. The collection became the restaurant's image. Today 25 to 50 percent of the collection travels from restaurant to restaurant.

PRICES

Albums/Album Covers

Beatles Autographed Album Cover. Blue ink autographs of all four Beatles: John Lennon, George Harrison, Paul McCartney, and Ringo Starr; on the back cover of the *Please Please Me* album; 12½ inches × 12½ inches; $1,725.

Beatles Autographed Album Cover with "Gold" Album. Boldly signed album cover for the Beatles' *A Hard Day's Night;* in blue ballpoint pen by George Harrison and John Lennon; matted and framed with a Paul McCartney autograph on off-white paper and a Ringo Starr autograph on white paper; with a "gold" copy of the album *A Hard Day's Night;* 25 inches × 17 inches; $2,530.

Beatles Autographs with Album Cover. All four Beatles' autographs on separate pieces of paper; Ringo Starr in blue ink on pink paper; John Lennon in black ink on gray paper; Paul McCartney in blue ink on gray paper; George Harrison in black in on blue paper; matted and framed with the *Sgt. Pepper's Lonely Hearts Club Band* album cover; 19 inches × 28½ inches; $1,955.

Awards

Beatles Original Certificate of Nomination from the Academy of Motion Picture Arts and Sciences, 1964. Presented to John Lennon and Paul McCartney for an Academy Award nomination in the category of outstanding achievement for best original sound score for *A Hard Day's Night* (1964); 10½ inches × 8½ inches; $9,487.

John Lennon Apple Records Award, 1968. Brass apple-shaped award inscribed "TO COMMEMORATE THE BEATLES 1ST APPLE SINGLE *HEY JUDE*, 4TH SEPTEMBER 1968"; mounted on a wooden base with a plaque inscribed "PRESENTED TO JOHN LEN-

Tee Shirts. Cotton, one with "The Beatles" and one with transfer portrait of the Fab Four and "The Beatles" printed above it; $10/each. Courtesy of Have A Nice Day.

NON"; serial number inscribed on the back "APPLE R 5722"; 4 inches high; $3,105.

John Lennon Autographed Card with "Gold" Single Award for *Instant Karma*. Felt-tip pen autograph with caricature drawing on the *Sometime in New York City '72* card; matted and framed with a "gold" single from *Instant Karma* and a large photo of John Lennon in front of the Statue of Liberty; 17 inches × 21 inches; $1,380.

Beatles "Gold" 45 Single Album Award for "I Want to Hold Your Hand." Early RIAA award presented to the Beatles to commemorate the sale of more than one million copies of the Capitol Records, Inc. single record "I Want to Hold Your Hand"; matted and framed; 17 inches × 13 inches; $2,990.

Photos

Beatles Autographed Color Magazine Photograph. Blue pen and ink autographed photo by all four members of the band; matted and framed; 17 inches × 19 inches; $1,725.

The Beatles. Black-and-white photograph; 4¼ inches × 6⅜ inches; $700.

Beatles Autographed Photograph, c. 1967. Blue felt-tip pen and black ballpoint pen autographs on a *Sgt. Pepper's Lonely Hearts Club Band* photograph; matted and framed; 15 inches × 16 inches; $1,725.

Beatles Autographed Publicity Photo. Blue felt-tip pen signatures on the photo that depicts all four Beatles holding teacups; in glass clip frame; 8¼ inches × 6½ inches; $1,955.

Miscellaneous

Large Collection of Beatles Memorabilia. Forty-seven assorted memorabilia comprising items such as Shea Stadium pennant, Disc-Go case, model kits, hummer, tray, stamps, pins, wallet, scarf, puzzle, sneakers, pillow, blow-up dolls, bath soap containers shaped like Paul and Ringo, John Lennon hanger, Beatles toy wig, books, etc.; $3,565.

John Lennon Signed Publishing Agreement for "Helter Skelter," October 15, 1968. Publishing agreement signed in black ballpoint pen by John Lennon as witness for the song "Helter Skelter"; discusses the percent distribution of royalties for the song; together with a photograph of Lennon and a plaque; $3,450.

Beatles Bobbing Head Figures, c. 1964. Set of four; $160/set.

Beatles Mirror, c. 1960s. Fab Four; 20 inches × 30 inches; $80.

Beatles Scrapbook with Mersey Beat Cuttings, All Four Autographs, Signed Paul McCartney Letter. Bound scrapbook includes Mersey Beat articles announcing the Beatles' recording for EMI; 11 pages covered with various articles all relating to the Beatles; with an early typed fan letter signed "Love Paul McCartney xxx"; with Paul McCartney autographed newspaper photo; also one page of pen-and-ink signatures by all four Beatles to a fan named Jenny; $2,185.

Beatles Autographs. Pen-and-ink autographs of all four

Toy, "Bobbing Head" dolls, made by Car Mascots, Inc., 1964. Four dolls, hand-painted, wearing gray-blue collarless suits, each plays appropriate instrument, on gold bases with fascimilie signatures; mint condition and boxed; doll height is 8 inches; $1,725. Courtesy of Sotheby's Inc.

Beatles on the Plaza Hotel stationery, inscribed "RINGO STARR/ PAUL MCCARTNEY (BEATLES)/JOHN LENNON/GEORGE HARRISON"; stationery is affixed to a cardboard page with a cut-out magazine photo of the Fab Four; $1,380.

John Lennon Series of Lithographs, Titled *Bag One*, 1970. Numbered limited edition comprising thirteen reproductions of drawings in sepia and ink, a poem, frontispiece, and explanatory page; each sheet numbered in pencil; fifteen sheets bearing pencil signatures of John Lennon; contained in white portfolio; 23 inches × 30 inches; $18,400.

John Lennon Signed Books (two). John Lennon's *In His Own Write* (first edition), signed on the inside cover in black ink; Yoko Ono's *Grapefruit*, signed at Claude Gil in 1971 by both John Lennon and Yoko Ono on inside cover in felt-tip pen; together with a snapshot photograph of Lennon; $1,380/set.

John Lennon Handwritten Lyrics for "Isolation." Black pen and ink handwritten lyrics; eight lines of "Isolation" on the back of an envelope and mounted on paper; offered with a color photograph of Lennon; 5½ inches × 9 inches; $3,450.

John Lennon and George Harrison Signed Checks. John Lennon's District Bank Limited check made out to Inland Revue for 1,500 pounds on January 7, 1969, and signed in black ballpoint pen on lower right, matted and framed with a photograph of John Lennon; George Harrison's National Westminster Bank, Ltd., check made out to Master Rentals Ltd. for 79 pounds, 75 pence on August 11, 1972, and signed in blue felt-tip pen on lower right, matted and framed with a photograph of George Harrison; both measure 22 inches × 13 inches; $1,725/set.

John Lennon, George Harrison, and Ringo Starr Signed Checks. John Lennon's District Bank Ltd. check made out to cash for 300 pounds on February 2, 1970, and signed in black ballpoint pen on lower right, matted and framed with a photograph of John Lennon; George Harrison's National Westminster Bank, Ltd., check made out to Burns, Burr & Company, Ltd., for 131 pounds, 99 pence on April 24, 1972, and signed in blue ballpoint pen on lower right, matted and framed with a photograph of George Harrison; Ringo Starr's National Westminster Bank, Ltd., check made out to Apple Films, Ltd. for 3,716 pounds, 8 pence on December 21, 1972, and signed in black ballpoint pen on lower right, matted and framed with a photograph of Ringo Starr; each measures 20½ inches × 15 inches; $2,300/set.

John Lennon Signed Publishing Agreement for "Back in the U.S.S.R.," October 15, 1968. Publishing agreement signed in black felt-tip pen by John Lennon as witness for the song "Back in the U.S.S.R."; discusses the percent distribution of royalties for the song; together with a photograph of John Lennon and a plaque; $3,565.

Large John Lennon and Yoko Ono Signed Caricature Drawing, 1969. Black marker on cardboard caricature drawing of both Lennon and Ono; inscribed "PEACE & LOVE, JOHN LENNON '69/YOKO ONO"; 22 inches × 28 inches; $9,775.

Original George Harrison Signed Script Page from *A Hard Day's Night.* Black ballpoint pen signature is inscribed "TO ALISON WITH LOTS OF LOVE FROM GEORGE HARRISON (LEARN YOUR LINES NEXT TIME)"; on the typed page 74 from the script for the 1964 film; the page is matted and framed with a photograph of Harrison along with a plaque; $1,265.

Beatles Autographs (two sheets). Pen and ink on paper; signed "JOHN LENNON/RINGO STARR/GEORGE HARRISON" on one sheet; signed "PAUL MCCARTNEY" on the other; both sheets are matted and framed with a copy of the *Sgt. Pepper's Lonely Hearts Club Band* album cover; 20 inches × 16 inches; $1,495.

Three Original Versions of the Beatles' Printer's Proofs for *The Beatles Yesterday and Today.* One double printer's sheet of the *Butcher* cover used for color registration (these proofs do not include the black print for the title and Capitol logo); single copy of the *Butcher* cover with print on heavier stock with rarely seen blue version of the album cover on a double printer's sheet used for color registration; together with the final version that was used as the *Butcher* cover (this shocking album cover has become one of the most sought-after collectibles due to the nature of the subject and the fact that it was later covered up by a more "appropriate" cover); $3,565.

❋ ERIC CLAPTON ❋

Eric Clapton "Platinum" Album Award for *Slow Hand.* RIAA award presented to RSO Records to commemorate the sale of more than one million copies of the RSO Records long-playing record album *Slow Hand;* matted and framed; 21 inches × 17 inches; $575.

PRICES

Three Doors Posters. The Doors 8/10–11/1967, poster from The Crosstown Bus, Brighton, Massachusetts (suburb of Boston); The Doors (plus many other bands) at Newport, California's Devonshire Meadows Fantasy Fair and Magic Music Festival, 7/15–16/1969; The Doors 2/14–28/1967, poster from the Whiskey A-Go-Go, San Francisco, California; $1,610/set.

The Doors "Gold" Album, Cassette, and CD Award for *L.A. Woman.* RIAA award presented to The Doors to commemorate the sale of more than 500,000 copies of the Elektra Records album, cassette, and CD; matted and framed; 21 inches × 17 inches; $1,265.

Fred W. McDarrah Original Photographs (two) of Jim Morrison and His Grave. A contemporary black-and-white print of Jim Morrison and The Doors at The Fillmore East, 105 Second Avenue, New York, March 22, 1968; and a contemporary black-and-white print of Jim Morrison's graffiti-marked grave in Cimetiere due Pere-Lachaise, Paris, photographed August 15, 1976; both are matted and signed by the photographer; both measure 20 inches × 16 inches; $690/set.

Jim Morrison Autograph. Black ballpoint pen signature inscribed on WFIL-TV Channel 6 stationery; $1,035.

❋ Bob Dylan ❋

PRICES

Fred W. McDarrah Original Photographs (two) of Bob Dylan. A contemporary black-and-white print of Dylan standing in Sheridan Square, New York, photographed January 22, 1965, for an article by Jack Newfield and published in *The Village Voice* concerning the LP *Highway 61 Revisited;* and a contemporary black-and-white print of Bob Dylan on the American

Tour with the band at the Spectrum in Philadelphia, Pennsylvania, taken January 6, 1974; both are matted and signed by the photographer, both measure approximately 21 inches × 16 inches; $1,380.

❋ JIMI HENDRIX ❋

PRICES

AWARDS

Jimi Hendrix "Gold" Album Award for *Are You Experienced?* RIAA award presented to Warner Bros. Records to commemorate the sale of more than 500,000 copies of the Reprise/Warner Bros. Records long-playing record album; matted and framed; 21 inches × 17 inches; $1,725.

Clothing

Jimi Hendrix Concert-Worn Pants, c. 1968. White cotton bell-bottom pants have an ornate blue embroidered floral pattern running the length of the right leg; lot includes a copy of the March 1988 issue of *Guitar World*, which features a photograph of Hendrix wearing the pants in concert (these pants were also worn by Hendrix at his famous Hollywood Bowl concert, where crazed fans jumped into the moat that was placed at the foot of the stage where Hendrix played); $16,100.

Miscellaneous

Jimi Hendrix Autograph with "Gold" Single for "Purple Haze." Blue ballpoint pen signature on paper inscribed "STAY GROOVY JIMI HENDRIX"; matted and framed with a "Gold" single for "Purple Haze" and a large photo of Hendrix; 17 inches × 21 inches; $2,530.

Jimi Hendrix Experience Autographed Poster, 1967. Inscribed by all three members of the band; Hendrix in blue ballpoint pen and inscribed "(BE) TO ARCHIE BE GROOVY JIMI HENDRIX"; in pencil "NOEL REDDING/MITCH MITCHELL"; the poster depicts all three on the tarmac at Heathrow Airport; glazed and framed; 18 inches × 24 inches; $1,035.

Jimi Hendrix Photographs (six), from Grona Lund, Stockholm, 1970. Series of six black-and-white photographs of Hendrix backstage at Grona Lund in Stockholm; photos include Hendrix performing, relaxing backstage, and backstage with his son by a Swedish woman; these photos were taken two weeks before his death; all photographs signed and dated; matted and framed; each photo measures 15 inches × 17 inches; $1,150.

Jimi Hendrix Autograph. Blue ballpoint pen signature inscribed on WFIL-TV Channel 6 stationery; $1,092.

Jimi Hendrix Handwritten Letter. Black ballpoint pen on lined paper inscribed "DEAR ELIZABETH, PLEASE EXCUSE ME FOR MAKING SUCH A VERY SHORT LETTER BUT WE MUST GO ON VERY SOON. BUT I REALLY APPRECIATE THE SWEET LETTER YOU GAVE ME—LOVE & KISSES FOREVER TO YOU. I WISH I COULD SEE YOU IN THE FLESH—I MEAN, IN PERSON. LOVE AGAIN TO YOU ALWAYS JIMI HENDRIX"; matted and framed with a photograph of Jimi Hendrix; 20 inches × 24 inches; $4,600.

Jimi Hendrix Handwritten Lyrics to the Song "Suddenly November Morning," c. 1968. Lyrics on Londonderry Hotel stationery in black felt-tip pen; inscribed "IT WASN'T . . . TOO LONG AGO SINCE I FELT . . . THE WARM HELLO OF THE SUN . . . WORK IN PROGRESS (in these lyrics, Hendrix writes of searching for a better place and time, with lyrics following more of a blues style); 11½ inches × 8¼ inches; $3,450.

Jimi Hendrix Handwritten Lyrics for the Song "Red Velvet Room," c. 1968. Two pages of white lined paper inscribed in black ballpoint pen; two complete verses of the song; lyrics include "THE JUKEBOX DIES, THE LIGHTS GO DOWN, THE SAWDUST FLOOR HAS CLAIMED THE LAST OF MY DRINKS—INTOXICATION MAKES MY EYES A FOOL AND MY BRAIN ALMOST CEASES TO THINK"; matted and framed with a black-and-white photograph of Jimi Hendrix; 21 inches × 25 inches; $14,950.

Jimi Hendrix Experience Autographs. Black felt-tip pen on lined paper; two autographed sheets of paper; the first is inscribed "LOVE ALWAYS JIMI HENDRIX" and the second is inscribed "LOVE! MITCH XXX NOEL REDDING"; both sheets matted and framed with a printed photo of all three; 18 inches × 14 inches; $2,070.

❋ JANIS JOPLIN ❋

PRICES

Album/Album Cover

Janis Joplin Autographed Album Cover. Blue felt-tip pen signature inscribed "LOVE JANIS JOPLIN" on the cover of Big Brother and the Holding Company album cover; matted and framed with a "Gold" copy of the album; 17 inches × 25 inches; $2,990.

Photos

Fred W. McDarrah Original Photographs (two) of Janis Joplin. A contemporary black-and-white print of Janis Joplin in performance at Bill Graham's Fillmore East, 105 Second Avenue, New York, February 11, 1969; and a contemporary black-and-white print of Janis Joplin with Big Brother and the Holding Company at Bill Graham's Fillmore East, August 1, 1968; both are matted and signed by the photographer; both measure 20 inches × 16 inches; $862.

Miscellaneous

Janis Joplin Autograph, c. 1969. Blue ballpoint pen autograph on off-white album sheet; inscribed "JANIS JOPLIN"; matted and framed with a photograph of Joplin holding a bottle; rare; 18 inches × 14 inches; $1,725.

Janis Joplin Autograph. Red pen and ink signature inscribed on WFIL-TV Channel 6 stationery; $920.

Tee Shirt, 1979. Imprint of KISS, 1979 World Tour and portraits of the group members, on the back "Security," black cotton with red, green, white, blue, manufactured by Aucoin; $125. Courtesy of Harvey Hesse Collection.

❋ KISS ❋

PRICES

KISS Concert-Worn Costumes, c. 1970s. Seven items; two sets of wrist cuffs, one worn by Peter Criss, the other worn by Ace Frehley, one neck choker, one waist belt, Gene Simmons's jock strap, some pieces with the Lagaspi label; together with five autographs of the band members, one folder, and two photographs; each costume item comes with a letter of authenticity from the band's publicity directory on KISS stationery; $3,220.

❋ LED ZEPPLIN ❋

PRICES

Led Zepplin Ampex Poster, 1969. Ampex advertisement poster for Led Zepplin's first album, *Led Zepplin*, on Atlantic

Records; featuring a two-tone photographic image of the band; 36 inches × 24 inches; $115.

❋ THE MONKEES ❋

PRICES

Collection of Monkees Memorabilia. Eighteen pieces such as a puzzle, child's T-shirt, paint set, lunchbox, thermos, *TV Guides*, binder, pins, mug, dolls, books, bracelet, playing cards, and more; together with a toy model for a Paul Revere and the Raiders coach; $920.

❋ MOTOWN AND R&B ❋

PRICES

Collection of Motown Memorabilia. Collection of pristine Motown sheet music for songs by artists such as Marvin Gaye, Martha Reeves and the Vandellas, the Jackson Five, the Four Tops, Diana Ross and the Supremes; includes English versions; ninety-six total; with collection of fifty-six editions of *Soul Magazine*, "America Most Soulful Newspaper," spanning 1968 to 1973; together with a cardboard Motown promotional stand-up in the shape of a record; $690.

❋ STEVIE NICKS ❋

PRICES

Stevie Nicks Autographed Tambourine and Publicity Photograph. Both items signed "MUCH LOVE STEVIE NICKS"; the tambourine in black with an added "ENJOY!"; the photograph is signed in gold ink; $632.

Stevie Nicks Signed Album, Cover, and Poster. Gold ink autographs on the album and cover; inscribed "MUCH LOVE STEVIE NICKS"; with a signed poster for Timespace; inscribed in black felt-tip pen "DREAMS AND GYPSIES, LOVE STEVIE NICKS"; $460.

Stevie Nicks Concert Banner. Large green nylon banner states "Sun Country Cooler & Westwood One Ratio Networks Present Stevie Nicks" (unlike store models used for promotion, this banner was displayed at the concert); 4 feet × 12 feet; $345.

❋ ELVIS PRESLEY ❋

PRICES

Clothing

Elvis Presley Jumpsuit, Cape, and Belt, c. 1972. Cream cotton jumpsuit with zipper front, flared trousers with lime-green inserts, high collar, and decorated with green, red, gold, and blue rhinestone sunburst design; label in the collar reads "NUDIE'S RODEO TAILORS"; a tag along the zipper has Elvis Presley's name and his chest size on it; together with silk-lined matching cape finished in dazzling rhinestone design and matching belt (this lot comes with a copy of the purchaser's invoice from Nudie's, who designed the suit, as well as a copy of an article about Nudie and his relationship with Elvis and other stars, and a photocopy of a picture of Elvis and Nudie); $17,250.

Elvis Presley Sunglasses. Rectangular aviator glasses with blue tint and stainless steel frames; made in Germany with the style "NAUTIC/NEOSTYLE" inscribed on the inside of the frame; $1,380.

Jewelry

Elvis Presley Lapis Lazuli Ring. Large 14K gold ring in a nugget style with a lapis lazuli stone mounted in the center; $6,900.

Elvis Presley "Gold" Engraved Cuff Link. Single cuff link with geometric design on one side of the link; engraved "EP" on the other (this lot comes with a certificate of authenticity from the Elvis Presley Museum signed by Elvis's aunt Della Mae); $920.

Miscellaneous

Elvis Presley "Gold" Key for Rolls-Royce. "Gold" key inscribed "ROLLS-ROYCE" with the Rolls-Royce logo; also inscribed "ELVIS PRESLEY"; $1,840.

Elvis Presley Portrait. Neon-accented; $152.

❋ QUEEN ❋

PRICES

Queen Autographed *A Night at the Opera* Album Cover. Boldly signed in blue felt-tip marker by all four members of Queen: Freddie Mercury, Brian May, John Deacon, and Roger Taylor; matted and framed; 15 inches × 15 inches; $977.

Queen Autographs with "Gold" *Queen II* Album. Red and black felt-tip pen autographs on paper for each band member: Freddie Mercury, Brian May, John Deacon, and Roger Taylor; matted and framed with a "Gold" album and cover for *Queen II*; 21 inches × 25 inches; $488.

❋ THE ROLLING STONES ❋

PRICES

Albums/Album Covers

Andy Warhol Signed Rolling Stones Album Promotion. Black pen signature inscribed "ANDY WARHOL" on the cover of the Rolling Stones album *Love You Live* promotional piece; matted and framed with a camouflage self-portrait of Warhol from 1986 (the cover for the album *Love You Live* was designed by Warhol in 1977); 18 inches × 14 inches; $1,380.

Photographs

Fred W. McDarrah Original Photographs (two) of Mick Jagger. Both contemporary black-and-white prints of Mick Jagger in performance at Madison Square Garden, New York, November 27, 1969; both matted and signed by the photographer; both measure 20 inches × 16 inches; $460.

The Rolling Stones Autograph. Pen-and-ink autographs on the centerfold photograph of *16 Magazine;* autographs include Mick Jagger, Bill Wyman, Keith Richards, Charlie Watts, and Brian Jones (this centerfold pullout was taken out of the magazine, so the balance of the magazine is not included); $488.

❁ BRUCE SPRINGSTEEN ❁

PRICES

Bruce Springsteen Handwritten Lyrics, c. 1971. Blue ballpoint pen on spiral notebook lined paper; the working lyric is titled "Sometimes at Night" and is written on both sides of the page; with a total of forty-three lines of lyrics; $920.

❁ MISCELLANEOUS ❁

PRICES

Assortment of Rock and Roll Autographs. Sixteen pen-and-ink autographs on photos, promo flats, and album covers; includes Prince, inscribed "LOVE GOD, PRINCE" and mounted with a photo, all members of Crosby, Stills, Nash and Young, all members of U2, Genesis, Aerosmith, Mick Jagger, Keith Richards, Bill Wyman, Rod Wood, Tom Petty, Janet Jackson, Mariah Carey, Yes, Huey Lewis, Cinderella, Terence Trent D'Arby; $1,380.

Collection of Autographed Album Covers and Photographs. Sixteen autographs in various inks and colors; includes Madonna, Kate Bush, Bruce Springsteen, Davie Bowie, Jerry Garcia, Eric Clapton, Pete Townsend, Jeff Beck, Lou Reed, Michael Bolton, Jon Bon Jovi, the Go Gos, the B52s, Aretha Franklin, Jethro Tull, and the Scorpions; $1,495.

World's Largest Backstage Pass Collection. Over 1,700

backstage passes comprised of laminates and satins, as well as radio passes; includes passes for stars and groups such as Madonna, Prince, Eric Clapton, Michael Jackson, the Allman Brothers, Billy Idol, the Beach Boys, Bob Dylan, Bruce Springsteen, Jimmy Buffet, Kiss, Melissa Etheridge, the Monkees, the Moody Blues, Ozzy Osbourne, the Pretenders, Wings, Queen, Rush, Stevie Nicks, Thompson Twins, Tom Petty and the Heatbreakers, Van Halen, the Tubes, the Who, Whitney Houston, Carole King, Cheap Trick, Crosby Stills and Nash, the Cult Heart, David Bowie, Elton John, David Lee Roth, Elvis Costello, Fleetwood Mack—just to name a few; this extensive collection is truly a study in backstage rock history; $3,450.

Bono Signed Acoustic Guitar. D-10N Washburn guitar, serial #92070042D; signed by Bono (of U2 fame) with bold caricature drawing of himself; both autograph and caricature are in blue felt-tip pen; $2,300.

Emerson, Lake, and Palmer Signed Guitar. D-10N Washburn acoustic guitar, serial #92070486D; six-string instrument with mother-of-pearl fret marks; inscribed boldly by Keith Emerson, Greg Lake, and Carl Palmer; inscriptions read "WELCOME BACK MY FRIEND" and "TO A LUCKY MAN BEST WISHES"; $1,495.

Legends of Rock Signed Guitar. D-10 Washburn acoustic guitar, serial #92109345; six-string instrument with mother-of-pearl fret marks, autographed by Tina Turner, George Michael, James Taylor, and Sting in bold blue marker; $977.

Eric Clapton, Ron Wood, and Brian May Signed Guitar. FG-410A Yamaha acoustic guitar, serial #90526371; mother-of-pearl fret marks; inscribed in bold ink by Eric Clapton, Ron Wood '92 (with caricature face), and Brian May '92; $3,220.

Collection of Signed Album Covers. Nine autographed album covers; includes Neil Young, *Comes a Time;* Crosby, Stills, Nash, and Young, *Déjà Vu;* the Rolling Stones, *Emotional Rescue;* Rod Stewart, *Every Picture Tells a Story;* Lou Reed, *Coney Island Baby;* Jethro Tull, *Too Old to Rock 'n' Roll, Too Young to Die!;* Elton John, *Ice on Fire;* David Bowie, *Young Americans;* and Roger Daltry, *McVicar for the Record;* $1,035.

Collection of Seven Movie Posters. Seven one-sheet posters include *When the Boys Meet the Girls; Twist All Night;* Chubby Checker in *Don't Knock the Twist; Monterey Pop; Teenage Millionaire; The Big TNT Show; Beach Ball;* each measures approximately 41 inches × 27 inches; $920.

Collection of Seven 1960s Rock Movie Posters. Includes *A Swingin' Summer*, with the Righteous Brothers, the Rip Chords, and many more; *The Girls on the Beach*, with the Beach Boys, the Crickets, and Leslie Gore; *Out of Sight*, with Gary Lewis and the Playboys, Freddie and the Dreamers, the Turtles, and many more; Sonny and Cher in *Good Times*; the Dave Clark Five; *The Big TNT Show*, with Ray Charles, Donovan, Petula Clark, the Byrds, and Lovin' Spoonful; *The Tami Show;* together with a wonderful French poster for the 1966 movie *Batman* and many others; $1,380.

Poster for the Shandells. $50.

Poster Collection. Seventy-two posters of Family Dog and Bill Graham, designed by artists such as Mouse, Kelly, etc., includes such musical groups as Jefferson Airplane, Greatful Dead; $3,737. Courtesy of Sotheby's Inc.

Poster, c. 1970. The Shandells, musical group; $50. Courtesy of Happy Face.

Poster, c. 1977. Elton John, signed James Grashow, published by Porta Publishing, Ltd., Porta Madera, CA, printed on chipboard; 27½ inches × 20 inches; $400. Courtesy of Skank World.

Silver and Other Metal Designs

Heading the list of prominent silver designers of the 60s and 70s is Georg Jensen, the award-winning Scandinavian silversmithy that celebrated its centennial in 1994. Their reputation for quality, innovative design work is well deserved. Designers of the era recognized for their work produced by the Georg Jensen include Soren Georg Jensen, one of the founder's sons, Henning Koppel, and Magnus Stephensen.

In England, industrial designer David Mellor used his training as a silversmith to produce high quality designs for everything from flatware to cooking utensils that were then mass produced.

While not noted here by specific example, many independent American silversmiths, whose primary work was jewelry, created small custom-made pieces such as bowls and vases that are just waiting to be discovered.

American Don Wallance made his mark through his use of new materials such as aluminum and stainless steel in the design of cooking and serving wares. His work is recognized by for the same qualities that distinguishes quality work in silver—a sculpted look with satin finish.

❋ SCANDINAVIAN DESIGNERS ❋

GEORG JENSEN SILVERSMITHY

The Georg Jensen Silversmithy celebrated its hundreth anniversary in 1994. It has kept its reputation for introducing new designs and using top designers over the years. Originally it made jewelry, but by 1915 it was producing flatware by such designers as Johan Rohde. By the early 1950s, Henning Koppel was creating Modern design hollowware, jewelry, and flatware. He was in the forefront in the 1960s and 1970s with the Postmodern look.

The silversmithy has received many awards over the years, and in 1980 its work was shown at the Renwick Gallery in Washington, D.C. Examples from the 1940s and 1950s were being snapped up by collectors in the 1970s. Prime examples from the past continue to rise in value.

Caryl Unger, a specialist and dealer of Georg Jensen silver, comments:

> Some problems for collectors are outright fakes and companies who take impressions of Jensen marks and apply them to other silver. The good news is that the marks ended up being reversed. So collectors should familiarize themselves with placement and types of marks. This happens with jewelry as well. I have even been taken—at a major auction. I found out it was a fake when I took the piece to be polished. Now that I look at it I realize the piece is too heavy and the marks are not quite right.
>
> Sometimes marks may be "different" but okay, such as when a piece goes through Paris. The mark will be "IMPORTE DE DENMARK" and be on the front of the silver. I always advise collectors to get the feel of a piece by holding it and studying the marks.
>
> There are many pieces of silver sculpture done in the 60s and 70s collectors should look for. For instance, Piet Hein is known for his "super eggs," small, egg-shaped boxes that can be held in your hand, done in 1960.

SOREN GEORG JENSEN (1917–   )

One of Georg Jensen's sons, Soren began his career as a silversmith but achieved his true success as a sculptor. Like his father, he trained at the Royal Academy of Art in Copenhagen. Following that he apprenticed at the Georg Jensen Silversmithy, completing his training in 1936. He succeeded his uncle, Gundorph Albertus, as director of production at the smithy. Later he became the artistic director. In 1946 he was awarded

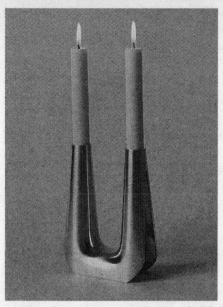

Candlestick designed by Soren Georg Jensen, 1963. Sterling silver; approximately 7 inches high; $51,200. Courtesy of Georg Jensen Museum, Copenhagen.

the Danish Gold Medal for his work. His silver has a sculptural feeling—very strong, sleek, and contemporary.

HENNING KOPPEL (1918–1981)

This Danish designer's background in drawing and stone sculpture included study at the Royal Danish Academy of Fine Arts in Copenhagen from 1936 to 1937, and at the Acadèmie Ranson in Paris in 1938. His interest in metals, first as a jewelry designer, began in 1940, when he went to Stockholm during the war. It continued when he returned to Copenhagen in 1945 to work with Georg Jensen Silversmithy on small pieces of jewelry. By the late 1940s and 1950s, when silver returned to the marketplace, he began creating hollowware. Today, these pieces are commanding top dollar at auction.

During the 1960s and 1970s his silver hollowware displayed his use of the graceful curves he had developed in the 1950s.

Many silver artists followed his lead in Europe and America. During this time he also designed jewelry, flatware, and sculpture.

This versatile artist also designed porcelain tableware for Bing and Grondahl, and glassware for Orrefors glassworks and Holmgaards, in Sweden, from 1971.

Among his many outstanding pieces are a fish dish and cover in silver for Georg Jensen from 1954 and a wine jug in silver for Georg Jensen from 1955.

His work has been exhibited in such museums as the Victoria and Albert Museum, London (1989); the Philadelphia Museum of Art (1983); and the Cooper-Hewitt Museum, New York (1982).

MAGNUS STEPHENSEN (1903–)

This Danish architectural and industrial designer studied at the Royal Academy of Fine Arts in Copenhagen from 1926 to 1930. While a free-lance designer from 1930, his commissions included furniture, textiles, metal, glass, and ceramics. His work in silver and stainless steel for Jensen is notable for clearly defined edges and strong curves. His work is in museum collections around the world.

Other Jensen silversmiths who worked in the 60s and 70s and are important to collectors include Jens Andressen, Piet Hein, Ole Ben Petersen, and Stephen Rostrup.

PRICES

Silver Vase, designed by Ole Kortzau for Georg Jensen, c. 1979. #1242; $5,800.

Silver Sculpture, designed by Ole Bent Petersen for Georg Jensen, c. 1979. $2,500.

Silver Sculpture, designed by Stephen Rostrup for Georg Jensen, c. 1979. $1,800.

Silver Tray, designed by Piet Hein for Georg Jensen, c. 1970s. $3,400.

Coffee Set with Matching Tray, c. 1970s. Danish silver; marked "COHR"; consisting of coffeepot, creamer, sugar bowl, and triangular tray of plain pear shape; with a Georg Jensen silver sugar spoon; 63 ounces; coffeepot 6½ inches high; tray 13⅜ wide; $2,530.

GUNNAR (CARL) CYRÉN (1931–)

As a student at the National College of Art and Design (1951–1956), Cyrén first studied silversmithing. Serving a silversmith apprenticeship for three years, he worked as a free-lance designer from 1956 to 1959. From 1959 to 1970 he created glassware as well for Orrefors glassworks in his native Sweden. Among the Orrefors pieces were his Pop wineglasses of 1965. By the mid-1970s he was working with silver again, as he does today.

❋ AMERICAN DESIGNERS ❋

DON WALLANCE (1909–)

This New York industrial designer studied at New York University from 1926 to 1930, receiving his B.A. in 1930. He also studied at the Design Laboratory, New York, from 1935 to 1939. From 1940 to 1941 he was design and technical director for the National Youth Administration in New Orleans, and from there went on to serve as a technologist in the United States Army in Washington from 1942 to 1943. The following years were spent as a free-lance designer specializing in metals, predominantly stainless steel. He was among the first to recognize the importance of using the new postwar materials and combining industry with craftsmanship.

Among his most important designs were his Forecast collection of cooking and serving wares in aluminum, for the Aluminum Corporation of America, 1962; and his hospital furniture in steel and plastics, for the Hard Manufacturing Company, 1965.

Collectors should look for his flatware (mentioned in the Jerryll Habegger price section). Among other important stainless steel flatware designs are:

- Palisander, in stainless steel and rosewood, originally made by H. E. Lauffer Company, 1969, now produced by Towle Manufacturing.

- Magnum, in stainless steel, originally made for H. E. Lauffer Company in 1970, now produced by Towle Manufacturing.

- Design 10, in colored plastics, originally made for H. E. Lauffer Company, 1971, now produced by Towle Manufacturing.

His designs can be recognized by their deeply forged, sculpted look and satin finish. They are also the hallmarks of fine silver.

PRICES

American Silver Three-Piece Coffee Set, Napier Company, Meriden, Connecticut, c. 1970. Comprising coffeepot on stand inset with teak panels and a nested spherical creamer and sugar bowl, fitting below; signed with initials "GS"; 27 ounces, is pennyweight gross; coffeepot on stand measures 8½ inches high; $1,035.

❀ ENGLISH DESIGNERS ❀

DAVID MELLOR (1930–)

Trained as a silversmith, this industrial designer has managed to combine craftsmanship with mass production. He studied at Sheffield College of Art from 1946 to 1948 and the Royal

---

College of Art, London, from 1950 to 1954. In 1954 he founded the David Mellor industrial design workshop, in Sheffield, specializing in cutlery. In 1969 he opened a shop in Sloane Square, London, where he sold cooking and eating utensils of his own design.

His work is in collections of the Victoria and Albert Museum, London; the Worshipful Company of Goldsmiths, London; the Museum of Modern Art, New York; the Philadelphia Museum of Art; and others.

Designs to look for include:

- Symbol flatware, for Walker and Hall. c. 1962.
- Embassy sterling silver flatware, for British Embassies, c. 1963.
- Provencal Stainless steel flatware, for David Mellor, c. 1973.
- Chinese stainless steel flatware, for David Mellor, c. 1975.
- Plane stainless steel flatware, for David Mellor, c. 1978.

❋ VARIOUS METAL SCULPTURAL DESIGNS ❋

PRICES

Male Torso, Alexandre Berrocal (1933– , Spanish), c. 1970. Edition of 1,000; signed and stamped "BERROCAL" and numbered "885/1000" on the base; 40 assembled bronze pieces; 5¼ inches high; very good condition; $400.

Mini-Davide, Alexandre Berrocal (1933– , Spanish), c. 1968. Edition of mini-multiples; a dismountable nickel-plated

Sculpture, designed by Aldo Turo, Milan, Italy, c. 1960s. Egg, parchment on wood; $400. Courtesy of Lost City.

Sculpture, c. 1960s. Copper and metal; 3 feet × 3 feet; $175. Courtesy Skank World.

aluminum alloy sculpture composed of multiple parts forming a male torso; signed "BERROCAL, 3833"; 5½ inches high; $385.

Mini-Maria, Alexandre Berrocal (1933– , Spanish), c. 1968. Edition of mini-multiples; a dismountable metal chrome sculpture composed of multiple parts forming a female torso; signed "BERROCAL, 1240"; 3 inches high; $350.

Sculpture, c. 1971. Patinated bronze head, stylized face, elongated earlobes, in the manner of a bodisattva, mounted on a black polished marble square plinth, incised "S.M. WRIGHT" (Stanton MacDonald-Wright); *height of bronze: 9½ inches; $1,100.* Courtesy of Butterfield and Butterfield Auctioneers.

❋ ❋ ❋

Textiles

For an overview of influences on the textiles people covered their furniture, floors, and windows with during the 60s and 70s, no one is a better qualified resource than internationally renowned designer Jack Lenor Larsen, who was responsible for many of the trends. In the late 40s and 50s he had already pioneered the then-new synthetic fibers. One special influence on his work was a 1947 meeting with contemporary weaver Dorothy Liebes, who also experimented with colors and synthetic fibers. In 1959 and 1960 Larsen became a consultant to the U.S. State Department on grass weaving in Taiwan and Vietnam. By 1968 he had opened the Jack Lenor Larsen International offices in Paris, Zurich, and Stuttgart. During the 1970s Thaibok Fabrics Ltd., an American firm founded in Bangkok in the 1940s, joined the growing Larsen group. Over the years he has won many awards and honors. He continues to influence contemporary design and has showrooms and production centers in thirty countries.

Jack Lenor Larsen, a textile designer, comments:

> The first youth of Modern design was spent before 1960. This was to be the last decade in which American design was dominant.
>
> The 1960s was a period of the new Establishment, of the rise of contract design, of the International Style, of the Miesian aesthetic of accelerating interest in prewar furniture design—often of chrome-plated tubes. There was considerable interest in controlling the glare and "night blackness" of the vast new windows of the modern houses and the curtain walls of the new high-rise towers. The casement fabric was ubiquitous.
>
> Large, unframed paintings in executive and residential interiors precluded competition from fabrics or carpets, and heavy wool textures became more common. Because the hand-

spun, undyed yarns were full of character in themselves, the weaves were simple. Stretch upholsteries were explored as a material to fit the new complex, compound curves of free-form furniture snugly. This was accelerated with the introduction of sculptural furniture by the French designers Olivier Mourgue and Pierre Paulin.

The influences of Art Nouveau and Tiffany continued, and the Japanese overtones of *House Beautiful* editor Elizabeth Gordon's "Shibui" promotion . . . the concept that "more was less" was considerable. When we longed for humanizing elements, architect and designer Alexander Girard filled this void with "popular artes" of Latin American.

The American-European interchange grew with exhibitions and with the ever-increasing number of continental publications and design fairs. The new generation of Scandinavian fabric designers included Rolf Middelboe, Verner Panton, and others. In Great Britain, especially at Heal's and Edinburgh Weavers, vibrant prints appeared. By the late 1960s we saw the first Ambiente fabrics by Finland's Timo Sarpaneva, "hand painted" by robot automata in two large Finnish cotton mills. There was also a second wave of Marimekko prints, these in the larger repeats and sure hand of Maija Isola.

We also experienced the ravages of psychedelia, the youth revolution, and the antiwar movement. Next came the breakdown of schools and civic institutions and with it a new freedom and abandon, most evidenced in apparel, but also in furnishings' patterns and colors. There was a new emphasis on the low-cost informality of floor pillows, soft furniture, and unconventional seating on forms inflated with air or filled with plastic beans. Who can forget the bean bag chair?

We saw for the first time a very considerable emphasis on highly styled linens. Following Everett Brown's pioneering (and unacknowledged) collections for Fieldcrest, sheets and towels were "in." We were hard at work on the highly styled first designer collections. Martex achieved classics; Spring Mills, an extraordinary Emilio Pucci group; and later, conservatively tasteful designs from the Bill Blass studio. We saw, too, a schizophrenic split between a youth-oriented, freewheeling residential market and the growing contract market, staid and Establishment in its point of view.

In the 1970s—the beige decade—we saw the popularization and exploitation of "natural" looks often inappropriate to the young families for which they were intended. There was a reaction against manmade fibers, and contract furnishings became so important as to dominate almost all new developments in furniture. We witnessed a national sophistication in which residents of even small towns experienced "gourmet" foods, modern dance, art films, and the effects of international travel.

In carpets we welcomed an end to the shag rug, the revival of smooth velvets and Wilton patterning, and—particularly in contract areas—the return to wools. There was a new sophistication in carpet making and patterning, and with it the development of needle-punching and other postindustrial techniques. The carpet tile became part of our repertoire.

Too often came "designer collections" put together under the banner name of some famous couturier or movie star; we heard of "fashion impulses." Eclecticism was rampant, and so was a nostalgia strangely new, and the erasing of many of the barriers between Modern and Traditional design. We saw the return of silk as an important fiber, of smooth damasks, Egyptian cottons, superimposed patterns, and the increasing importance of Art Deco.

A merger of European and American design was typified by the fresh new prints of Sven Fristedt of Sweden and the renewed popularity of Marimekko. Jack Larsen's first Thaibok silk collections introduced brocades, "ikats," and discharge printing. The palette of the decade was low-keyed, soft, and "adult," which produced in the mass market too many undyed, soil-prone yarns.

Art fabrics—sometimes tapestries, but more often bold experiments hung from walls and ceilings or supported on pedestals—became important elements in public spaces. All through the decade we experienced environmental concerns, questions of reuse, recycling, and restoration. These same concerns are still with us and will doubtless influence designs and fabrics in the coming decades.

❁ Textiles and Wall Coverings ❁

Artist and designer Jack Denst introduced the first free-hanging murals and silk-screened designs on steel, glass, and acrylic. He has always been a trendsetter, and came into prominence with his bold, contemporary wall covering designs of the late 40s. His awards include twenty-two from A.S.I.D. alone for design and technique. His work has been shown at New York's Metropolitan Museum of Art and the Victoria and Albert Museum in London, as well as at the Chicago Design Center, which put on a one-man show of his wall coverings. He has issued over twenty collections of silk-screened wall coverings and murals and was largely responsible for the renewed interest in wall coverings in the 60s and 70s.

Mr. Denst comments:

> Back in 1947 I opened a studio in my father's basement, and with the $10,000 I had saved from my army pay, I designed thirteen books of wallpaper designs—very stylized and in the Modern mode. I took the books first to Warner wallpapers. They turned it down. "We don't want that stuff," they said, and advised me to find another profession. So I took the patterns and built thirteen books. My friends did the selling and sold them all in a couple of weeks. I did all the designs by hand. When we first got orders we bought plain wallpaper from local paint stores. Marshall Fields and other big-name stores wanted the designs Warner had rejected.
>
> From the beginning I treated my wall coverings as fine art. I signed everything like the Chinese did; I hid my signatures among the designs. I also gave my designs names, like artists did. One of my most popular designs was titled "Beyond the Path You Can See the Sky." One of my murals from the 60s was titled "Promise I'll See Freedom." I did my first mural around 1954 because I wanted something larger to express myself than the repeat patterns. I liked using a variety of materials for my murals. At one time or another I've used silk screen on steel, copper, glass, and acrylics. The panels

were four by eight feet and were first exhibited
at the Design Center in Marina City Towers in
Chicago. I think we've used just about every material except burlap.

Since Denst's wall coverings and murals were sold all over
the United States as well as internationally, examples can turn
up anywhere. Full books of wallpapers or single swatches are
collectible. Examples of all his wall coverings can be seen at
the Chicago Historical Society.

BEN ROSE (1916–   )

The singular forty-seven-year career of Ben Rose, one of the
few truly influential pioneers in the field of contract textiles,
was documented in a special display at Chicago's Merchandise
Mart in 1993, commemorating his fortieth anniversary as a tenant there.

He was a fine arts major at the Art Institute of Chicago
from 1939 to 1943. Like many of his contemporaries, Ben Rose
was inspired by the influential painters of the day, such as
Picasso, Miró, and Klee, as well as by the architecture and
spare interior design of architect Mies van der Rohe.

His career began in 1946, when he presented an architect
friend (Henry Glass) with a set of hand-printed place mats he
and his wife had designed. Impressed, Glass asked him to create some print patterns for the first building he built in Chicago
after World War II. At the time there were very few contemporary printed fabrics available. Encouraged, Rose and his wife,
Frances, along with Helen Stern, formed a company and created some print designs, showing them to residential showroom representatives in Chicago's Merchandise Mart.

By the end of 1946 he had won his first design award—an
A.I.D. Honorable Mention for a printed fabric he called
"Chinese Linear." In 1947 he designed sixty yards in a Hawaiian
print for the first United Air Lines Stratocruiser flight from

Wall covering, "Mykonos I," Ben Rose design, Ben Rose production, c. 1970s. Inspired by the Greek Agean island of Mykonos, horizontally striped pattern is made up of alternating bands of color representing the sunlit seaside below a row of white-washed churches enclosing colorful doorways and topped by a dome-shaped skyline. Courtesy of Ben Rose Designs Inc.

Chicago to Hawaii. The resulting publicity started him on his successful lifetime career.

Among his many firsts were that he designed fabric for the first covered refrigerator door in 1952. In 1953 he designed a special group of linear prints for Packard Motors, and received the "Order of Leopold II of Belgium" for promoting Belgium linen in the United States. In 1952 and 1953 the Walker Art Center opened with a landmark textile exhibit. Along with the work of other top designers such as Alexander Girard and Angelo Testa were examples of Ben Rose's work. Following the exhibit he opened his first Merchandise Mart showroom and is today in the same space. Throughout the 60s and 70s his designs evolved with the changing tastes to include Op and Pop and the bold color combinations of those decades.

His designs can be seen in the collections of the Museum of Modern Art in New York, the Houston Contemporary Art Association, the Walker Art Center, the Art Institute of Chicago, the Museum Des Artes Decoratif in Montreal, the Rhode Island School of Design, and the permanent collection of Cooper Union in New York.

Ben Rose comments:

> I'll never forget the first time we tried to sell our designs to the residential showroom people in Chicago's Merchandise Mart. We were politely shown the door with remarks like "We've had wild stuff like this before. It didn't sell then and it won't sell now." Fortunately we didn't pay any attention.
>
> My wife and I set up a small print table (thirteen yards long) in a loft space we paid $75 a month for. Most hand-screened printing is done with two printers on either side of the table. As I was the only printer, we had to make screens half the width of the table that were joined when I ran around the other side of the table to print.
>
> Henry Glass became our first client. He wanted simple, abstract patterned drapery fabrics for his three-story art studio. Our plan was to set up a temporary factory to accommodate his 3,000-yard print order and to use the proceeds to set up a storefront gallery and studio where we could survive as fine artists. Due to material shortages after World War II, it took over a year to produce the order. In the meantime, Fran took samples of our patterns to several interior designers and we began to get small

orders, which forced us to create a business we hadn't really planned on.

There was very little abstract design being screened on fabric in 1946, the year we began. At the time screen printing consisted of hand-cut stencils affixed to frames stretched with porous silk fabric. This resulted in hard-edged, simple patterns in two or three colors. About two years later, photographic emulsions were developed that allowed subtle, textural effects, which influenced the design process.

In the early days, before inexpensive design copyrights were available, our patterns were "knocked off" regularly. Copyrights were sold

Textile, Ben Rose design, c. 1966. Drapery, Pop Art motif, "Tenayuca," one print color. Courtesy of Ben Rose Designs Inc.

for over $200 and didn't protect you from copycats who made the most minor of changes. Today, copyrights cost $7.50 and are quite strongly protective.

I believe that creating a surface design is like producing a building material as functional in its visual expression as bricks, mortar, and stone are structurally. The printed designs represent a constant searching for the balance in line, mass, and scale as a textural unit and its relation to other textures in the space structure.

In the past ten years, with the proliferation of jacquard looms, we have concentrated on upholstery fabrics. The jacquard technology allows one to create woven designs unlimited in pattern, scale, and texture.

Recently the health care market (which is where most of our print patterns were sold) has enjoyed a resurgence in activity and is becoming an important area of business for us. We plan to reintroduce many of our designs from the 40s and 50s that are still contemporary . . . especially for pediatric areas.

MARIMEKKO OY

This world-famous Finnish textile company, initially founded as Printex in 1949 by Viljo Ratio, became Marimekko in 1966. Designer Armi Ratia, who established Marimekko, quickly hired such top artists as Maija Isola and Liisa Suvanto. As such it became a European trendsetter with young adults who found the bold patterns and colors the perfect foils for their Postmodern furnishings. Americans became aware of Marimekko when Jacqueline Kennedy bought dresses made of Marimekko fabrics.

Vivid, unlikely color combinations and supergraphics typify the textile designs. Many patterns were designed by Maija Isola.

The company is still making everything from clothing to wallpaper and linens.

For an idea of what to look for, what follows are pages reprinted from a 1975 Crate and Barrel catalog. Since they still carry Marimekko items, a visit to one of their stores around the country, or their catalog, will give an idea of their distinctive look. The original 60s and 70s designs can turn up anywhere . . . from vintage clothing stores to thrift shops and estate sales.

One piece of Marimekko fabric is a reflection of the people of Finland. Their obsession with color. Their mania for architecture and design. Their compulsion to dance whether they're happy or sad. Their delightful love of flowers and nature.

In Finland, a cold, harsh climate wraps everything in a somber, sunless gloom for three months of the year.

So, when the first yellow wildflower pushes its way relentlessly through the snow, it is appreciated. When the first raw colors of a temporary spring begin to dot the landscape, they are cherished.

This love of color makes Marimekko unique. Color gives character to Marimekko. Sometimes in broad sweeping strokes of one color. Sometimes in tiny, dancing accents of many colors.

Color combinations can be as naive as a child's painting or subtly sophisticated.

They can be as sun-filled as a Paul Klee canvas. Yellow gold on brilliant orange. Hot pink on bittersweet.

They can be as somber as a winter landscape. Sea-green on violet. Black on moanberry. Magenta on plum.

Some of the fabrics are intricately patterned. Some are bold, free, and loose. Some are severe and geometric.

Every yard of Marimekko fabric is hand silk-screened. The result is a one-of-a-kind.

A Marimekko wall hanging is like an original work of art. A pillow, bedspread, tablecloth, napkin, stuffed animal, or shower curtain made by Marimekko is a statement of its owner's individuality.

In addition to being happy, flower-loving, and design conscious, the Finns are demanding.

In a country with one of the highest standards of living in the world, where a gallon of gas costs $1.50, everything has to last a long time.

That's why when Marimekko introduced a line of bags in Finland last year, they were as well made and practical as they were beautiful.

The bags are made from the most rugged type of canvas duck.

They're washable, colorfast, and water repellent.

They're big.

—Reprinted from the 1975 Crate and Barrel
catalog by permission

LENORE TAWNEY (1925–)

This fiber artist was first educated at the Art Institute of Chicago from 1946 to 1948. Her interest in mysticism led her first to Paris, then to Africa and the Near East. She then studied tapestry weaving with Martta Taipale at the Penland School of Crafts in North Carolina. After moving to New York in 1957 she used fetishistic pre-Columbian textiles for inspiration, and tied shells and feathers into her fringes. In the 60s she began the large, three-dimensional woven sculptures that she is best known for. During this same period she created one of her most important public artworks, two stories high, *Cloud Formations.*

❀ VARIOUS TEXTILE DESIGNS ❀

PRICES

Tapestry, after Robert Motherwell (1915–1991, American), c. 1965. Blue and green wool tapestry; woven with initials "RM" in lower right; exhibited in New York, Charles E. Slatkin Galleries, Inc., Contemporary Tapestries, 1968, no. 16 (another example); 113½ inches × 98 inches; $1,000.

English Wool Rug, designed by Mobley, #24, c. 1960. Abstract musician figure in black, mustard, red, and silver metallic thread on gray field; 85 inches × 37 inches; $275.

Carpet, Edward Fields. Unusual triangular winged form of sculpted multicolored shapes in red, black, white, browns, and beige; 142 inches × 142 inches × 180 inches; excellent condition; $1,100.

Carpet, Edward Fields, c. 1960. Rectangular carpet in soft beige with subtle leopard print pattern; 60 inches × 94 inches; excellent condition; $125.

Rug, Nichols. Off-center black and cream divided background with triangular and diamond geometric composition; 48 inches × 84 inches; excellent condition; $250.

Shag Rug, Verner Panton. Mira Romantica; graduated square design; earth tones of brown and orange; 78 inches × 55 inches; excellent condition; $140.

Toys

The postwar generation, known as the baby-boomers, was the first to own a television set and was also catered to by toy manufacturers. As a result television was used as a tool to sell toys to youngsters via Saturday morning cartoons and other children's programs. Important toys were developed from the cartoons, among them the Flintstones and Yogi Bear merchandise. Toy shelves were loaded with space toys, monster toys, plastic and battery-operated toys, wind-ups, and merchandise spun off from the cartoon world of Hanna-Barbera. Since this category is covered extensively in other books, I have listed only a few examples, among them the trendsetting Barbie doll.

If you are interested in collecting toys from the 1960s and 1970s, do it now, before prices begin to skyrocket as they did for toys from the 1940s and 1950s. Some examples are already fetching more than $300. However, this doesn't mean every toy made in the 60s and 70s is a collectible, priced fairly, or destined to rise in price over the next two decades. Tastes change over the years, just as they do in other categories of collecting.

Focus on a single area, such as model kits, television personalities, cartoon character merchandise, or celebrity figures. Rock group toys and monster toys, along with battery-operated cars, are popular at the time of this writing. Battery-operated toy cars of the 60s came from a variety of makers. There was a comic musical cat from Nomura, Japan; the Desert Patrol jeep from Modern Toy; Mister Magoo car from Hubley; and the popular Batmobile from 1966, made of blue metal. Included with it were the plastic figures of Batman and Robin.

❋ THE BARBIE DOLL ❋

Barbie could be called the doll that changed doll history. Introduced at the New York Toy Fair in 1959, she was an original, molded of hard vinyl. Introduced as "Barbie Doll, Teen-Age Fashion Model," she had only a few items of clothing. She was the creation of Ruth Handler, who originally made her for her own little girl. It was Ruth's husband, Elliot, and his partner,

Toy. Robbie the Robot, plastic; 3 inches high; $30. Courtesy of Skank World.

Banks. White metal: rocket, $30; flying saucer, $25. Courtesy of Skank World.

Harold "Matt" Matson, who ran a small toy company and decided to produce Barbie. She was launched by Mattel Toy Company. Since then, over 600 million Barbies and Barbie line products have been sold.

IDENTIFYING EARLY BARBIES

Barbies 1 and 2 were representative of the fashions of the day. Both had ponytails and curly bangs. The irises of their eyes were painted white and their dark eyebrows resembled an inverted V. Barbie 1 wore hoop earrings and had holes in her feet to fit the prongs on her round stand. Barbie 2 had a new type of stand that did not require holes in the doll's feet; instead, a stand with a tall wire back fit under her arms. Barbie 2 wore pearl stud earrings.

Barbies 1 and 2 can sell in shops for between $1,000 and $2,500, depending on the condition and the number of original accessories they have.

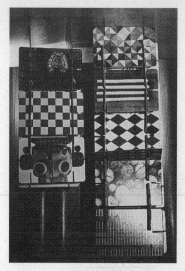

Robot. c. 1960s. Made for General Motors for use in three television commercials, then used in auto show displays; $1,800. Courtesy of Modern Times.

Giant House of Cards, designed by Charles and Ray Eames, manufactured in West Germany for Creative Playthings, c. 1960s. Second of three variations with thirty beautifully illustrated graphic designs in original box; each card measures 5 inches × 7 inches; $600. Courtesy of Toomey-Treadway Galleries, Oak Park, IL.

BARBIE'S BOYFRIEND, KEN

Ken was created in 1961 to be Barbie's boyfriend. He was named after Ruth and Elliot Handler's son and became an instant collectible. With his own swinging fashion wardrobe, he has been with Barbie ever since. When Barbie went to Woodstock in 1969, Ken was also appropriately dressed with fringed clothing. In 1975, when a Gold Medal Barbie wore athletic attire, Ken was decked out as a skier, displaying his own fashions and Olympic Gold medal.

IDENTIFYING KEN

The first Ken had fuzzy flocked hair. His body, clothed in red swim trunks, was made of hollow hard plastic. He was marked "KEN/PATS. PEND/MCMLX/BY MATEL, INC."

Barbie Doll, produced by Mattel, c. 1958. Molded hard vinyl; 11½ inches high; $2,800. Courtesy of a private collector.

❋ MISCELLANEOUS TOYS ❋

PRICES

Dolls

Action Figure, Odd Job, Gilbert, c. 1965. Plastic doll with spring-activated arm that throws derby; with box; box measures 12 inches × 5 inches × 4 inches; doll 12 inches high; near-mint condition; $129.

Beatles Dolls. Set of four; stuffed cloth; $175/set.

Cher Doll. Hair "grows"; MIB (mint condition in box); $35.

Fred Flintstone Doll, c. 1970. Vinyl with cloth clothing; marked "HANNA-BARBERA PRODUCTS, DAKIN"; $50.

Figure, c. 1960s. Caricature protester with long fake fur hair; holds protest sign; 5 inches high; $40.

Ken with Straight Legs, 1961. $50.

Ken with Bending Legs, 1962. $20.

Lunch Boxes

Bee Gees Lunch Box, c. 1978. Metal; $48.

Bionic Woman (Lindsay Wagner) Lunch Box. Metal; $50.

Happy Days Lunch Box. Metal; $48.

Model Kits

Addams Family Haunted House, by Aurora/Filmways, #805, c. 1965. All plastic assembly kit; with instructions and unused cardboard sheet with printed windows for house; marked "C8/9"; original box; $595.

James Bond and Odd Job, by Airfix/Gildrose, c. 1966. With plastic model assembly kit and instructions; $1/12$ scale; box with lid 6 inches × 9 inches; $193.

Rat Patrol, by Aurora, c. 1967. Includes HO-scale Rat Patrol jeeps with figures, two German Panzer tanks, German soldiers, sand dunes, and palm trees; unassembled; $189.

Surf Fink Model, by Revell, c. 1964. Includes all-plastic assembly kit of monstrous Fink; unassembled; boxed; box measures 9 inches × 6 inches; near-mint condition; $249.

Miscellaneous

Monkees Automobile, ASC, Japan, c. 1960s. Shows the GTO convertible; includes tin-and-plastic car with singing group figures inside; friction-powered motor and battery-operated recording about the vehicle; with box; car measures $11\frac{1}{2}$ inches long; box measures 13 inches × 6 inches × 4 inches; $505.

Batman Compass. With wristband; $50.

Jukebox, c. 1966. Rock-Ola; $1,195.

Bathroom Scale. Charlie the Tuna; $45.

Ladies' Platform Shoes, 1960s. Silver lamé; $50.

Flintstone's Truck and Trailer, Linemar, c. 1961. Tin friction toy; lithograph truck shows the cartoon figures; original box; 12 inches long; $3,200.

Wood

Rarely do handcrafted wooden objects come to auction, or to the booths of dealers specializing in mid-century modern items. They turn up mostly in consignment and thrift shops. Even though I haven't been able to list prices, I feel wood pieces are important and overlooked examples of Modern design and certainly something for collectors to consider.

In the 1950s, it was the Danish designers who began to highlight the beauty of wood through its use in their utilitarian objects. From turned wood bowls to pepper mills, they changed the way we entertained and the look of our dining tables. You probably take the ritual of tossing the salad in a handsome wood bowl for granted, nor do you consider the beauty of a wooden pepper mill. But it wasn't until Dansk International Designs began production in 1954 that the salad bowl came to the table, along with many of their other products from glassware to stainless steel flatware.

It was Ted Nierenberg, an American, who founded Dansk, when he recognized the need for objects befitting the laid-back life-style of the postwar decade. Among the designers working

Shallow Wooden Bowl, designed by Tapio Wirkkala, Finnish, c. 1950–1960. $400. Courtesy of Al Eiber Collection.

for Dansk was Jens Quistgaard. His ice bucket, considered a classic, is worth hunting down.

Well-known Danish furniture designer Finn Juhl also tried his hand at woodworking. He fashioned bowls from solid blocks of teak that dramatized the grain of the wood. The bowls and other examples of Danish woodwork had a finish of rubbed oil rather than varnish. They could be used indefinitely without refinishing, the same concept that made Scandinavian furniture popular. Oil finishes meant pieces could simply be refurbished rather than refinished.

Dansk Designs signatures are branded on the bottom of pieces.

Danish woodenware rode a wave of popularity in the 1960s and 1970s and the public became aware of many designers who are now collectible. One, Richard Nissen, was introduced to the American market at the Crate and Barrel store. In the following reprint from a Crate and Barrel 1975 catalog, Nissen describes how the finest woodenware is made in Denmark.

> My grandfather, whose name was also Richard Nissen, started our firm in 1890.
>
> He was a cooper. He made barrels and sold them to many places in this part of Denmark.
>
> Our staving technique really began with those barrels. My grandfather taught my father the process and he then taught me when I was fifteen. The same is true for many of the people here. Most are second- or third-generation workers. Some have worked here for forty years.
>
> We still manufacture the barrel staves and heads, but most of our business is now making bowls, boards, and trays.
>
> We began doing this in the early 1950s. At that time, as you know, Scandinavian design was beginning to have its influence on the home. Our simple wooden shapes began to take the

place of other more ornate pieces that had always been made of other materials.

There is a certain amount of what you would call "Old World" charm to our business. There is a discipline and a sense of craftsmanship and quality that we possess. But our pride is how we have taken this craftsmanship further with technological means.

We, of course, start with the wood. For many years, the forest around Langaa here provided the raw timber—the native beech and pine. These are beautiful, simple woods.

About twenty-five years ago, we also started working with teak imported from Siam. Teak was no stranger to us here in Denmark. Some of our finest sailing ships were made of teak because the wood is so hard and durable.

We liked the Siamese teak because it was almost exotic. The grain never seems to be the same. It even improves with age. As this salad bowl is used, the grain becomes more pronounced and the color gets deeper and richer.

The wood arrives here as trimmed logs. The log is cut into boards and the boards into long staves, one inch thick and two inches wide.

The staves are cut by what I think is the only automated sawmill in the world. We designed and "homemade" it.

It takes about three weeks to kiln-dry the staves. The kiln is operated day and night with high-velocity air and steam radiators until the moisture content of the staves is exactly 7 percent. Then they're stored in an airtight warehouse to maintain the low moisture content.

We now make what the old coopers would call a tub. The stave is shaped with a conical joint and the angle has to be very accurate to make a perfect cone. We are careful at this point that the staves are all of assorted colors and grains so the finished product will be more interesting.

We use an epoxy resin to glue the staves together. There is no question in the workers' minds that this had to be done perfectly or the piece would be worthless.

After the glue has cured the tub is put in a lathe and a groove, called a croze, is turned for the bottom.

The bottom, also made up of staves, is turned to fit the croze and glued with the staves.

Different lathes then form the inside and the outside profile. Now it is a salad bowl. All that remains are dozens of sanding, lacquering, oiling, and polishing steps.

—Reprinted from the 1975 Crate and Barrel
catalog by permission

❀ AMERICAN STUDIO ART WOODENWARE ❀

It wasn't until the late 1970s that professionally turned wood objects were collected seriously and pieces found their way to American art galleries. They still weren't considered suitable acquisitions for art museum collections. One of the first to break that tradition was the Phoenix Art Museum. Up until this time, turned wood objects were the stuff of craft galleries, or were considered strictly utilitarian. Now, works of master turners such as Rude Osolnik and James Prestini are seriously collected in the same way people collect the work of studio art glass and ceramic artists. Their work is also represented in museum collections that include the National Museum of American Art, the Smithsonian Institution, the Renwick Gallery, the National Museum of American Art, and the Art Institute of Chicago.

By exploiting the beauty of wood grain and exploring new forms, these artists have opened up a new category for collectors. Each of the following artists is known for specific techniques, choice of woods, and forms.

JAMES PRESTINI (1908–   )

Considered one of the greatest American masters of wood turning, James Prestini began turning pieces in 1933 and continued into the 1970s. His education included a degree in mechanical engineering from Yale University's Sheffield Scientific School. But it was as a math teacher at Lake Forest Academy, in Lake Forest, Illinois (1933–1942), that he began making lathe-turned wood bowls. It was when he began teaching as a craftsman at the Chicago School of Design (1939–1946) in collaboration with Moholy-Nagy, an artist, that interest in wood turning as an art form began to grow. But it was the 1950 exhibit of his work at the Museum of Modern Art in New York that brought him to the attention of the public. He created the Architecture Design Laboratory at the University of California at Berkeley.

Other designers include:

- David Ellsworth—David Ellsworth is known for his wooden vessels that use any part of a tree from burl to roots.
- Ronald E. Kent (Honolulu, Hawaii)—His most common forms are bowls and bottles of Norfolk Island Pine, a tree growing in Hawaii and throughout the South Pacific.
- Melvin Lindquist—This pioneer is known for creating new tools and turning techniques.
- Ed Moulthrop—Ed Moulthrop is recognized for his skill in bringing out wood's beauty, grains, and colors with simple shapes and polishing techniques.

Vessel, created by Rude Osolnik, master wood turner, c. 1970s. Redwood lace burl vessel, prices for his 1970s work range from $3,000 to over $5,000. Courtesy of Banaker, Gallery, SF.

- Rude Osolnik—This artist has the remarkable skill of being able to develop wood defects into beauty on his lathe. His forms are simple and the wood he uses can include everything from burls to laminated pieces.

❋ WOOD TOYS ❋

By the late 50s Scandinavian toys made of wood were introduced to the American market. Their manufacture continued in the 1960s and 1970s. Sparse of line and often brightly painted, they were in keeping with the Modern look. Doubtless because they were sturdily made, many have survived rough-and-tumble times. Everything from pull toy trains to blocks were produced, and they are worth looking for. They were expensive toys in their day.

Glossary of
Glass Terms

AIR BUBBLES   Used for decorative purposes, most often in Scandinavian glass.

ANNEALING   The process of placing a glass piece in a chamber of the furnace in order for the glass to cool after forming, thus reducing brittleness in the glass and making it stronger.

APPLIED DECORATION   A type of relief ornamentation made by adding glass threads, blobs, prunts, and other motifs to the piece's surface.

BLOW PIPE   A long and hollow iron rod approximately $5\frac{1}{2}$ feet long. The thick end is used to gather a blob of molten glass, the other has a mouthpiece used for the blowing process that shapes the hot glass into the desired size or form.

CASED GLASS   A glass piece consisting of two or more fused layers of different colors, often decorated by cutting them so that the inner layers show through. It is also referred to as case glass.

COLD PAINTING   The use of lacquer or oil-based pigments to create a color design on the glass without subsequent firing.

ENAMEL   A glass composition applied by fusion at a fairly low temperature. It is often used in powdered form to decorate the surface of metalwork, glass, or pottery.

ENGRAVING   The use of several types of tools to decorate the glass surface. Wheels are used in wheel engraving and sharp or diamond-pointed tools are used to produce linear patterns, dotted-stipple engraving, and diamond-point engraving.

ETCHING   A decorative technique that incises the surface or makes it shiny, matte, or frosted by exposing the piece to hydrofluoric acid.

FIRE POLISH   A finish given to the surface of glass that has lost some its surface smoothness from having been worked on. This is done by putting the piece back into the furnace in what is called the glory hole, which is an opening made expressly for this purpose.

FLASHING The process of coating a glass piece with a thin layer of either colored or clear glass to achieve a particular effect.

FLUX A chemical substance, such as potash, lead, or soda, that is used to lower the melting point of the main silica constituent of the glass material.

FREE-BLOWING The forming of objects on the blow pipe by blowing and manipulating hot, ductile glass.

GRAAL TECHNIQUE A type of glass originating in the Orrefors glass house in Sweden. Etched or cut designs in a colored layer of glass are placed over the original piece. The piece is then reheated and covered with a flashing of colorless glass.

LEAD CRYSTAL Clear and colorless glass fluxed by the use of lead oxide.

MARVERED LAMPWORK Glass made by manipulating tubes and rods in the flame of a lamp or burner. A marver is a metal slab on which the glass is gathered and rolled into the desired shape or smoothness.

METAL Glass that is in a molten state.

MIXED MEDIA A combination of substances, such as metals, used in glass decoration.

MOLD BLOWN Glass that is blown into a mold to create both the pattern and shape.

OVERLAY An ornamental veneer of either colored or clear glass that is placed over the original piece. Similar to cased glass.

PATE DE VERRE A technique that melts down already powdered glass into a mold.

PRUNT A decorative pad of glass applied to the wall of a vessel and usually drawn out into a thornlike projection or stamped with a die to create a pattern of raised dots.

SANDBLASTED   A decorative technique of exposing glass to a blast of sand in order to create a matte or frosted surface.

SLUMPING   A "warm" technique done in the kiln, where temperatures do not reach those needed in the furnace for glassblowing. It was developed in the 1970s.

STIPPLING   A decorative technique in which the glass surface is tapped gently with a pointed instrument to create a design and tonal effects with tiny dots.

Glossary of
Plastic Terms

It was the introduction of new plastic materials and forming methods that enabled designers of the 1960s and 1970s to create an amazing variety of designs for plastic furniture and household objects. One innovation was molded polyurethane (foamed plastic). Another was the use of the injection-molding process for making furniture, the process used to create the Marilyn sofa. The following glossary highlights some of the most important developments and is followed by a list of identifying trademarks.

ABS STRONG   A nonreinforced plastic with a high gloss to both sides of a finished piece. Used to make injection-molded furniture. It was first introduced in 1967 when Joe Columbo designed the first injection-mold, four-leg stacking chair. It was made by Kartell and is composed of styrene, acrylonitrile, and butadiene.

ACETATE   Cellulose acetate. Invented by the French scientist Henri Dreyfuss in 1900, it was developed for use by the DuPont de Nemours Company as early as 1906. Near the end of the 1920s its versatility was beginning to be discovered. It was spun into early rayon fabric and was also used in a hard form to produce a nonflammable coating for automobile and airplane bodies. Later, as cellulose acetate, it was used in doorknobs and eyeglass frames. In sheet form it could be made into lamp shades.

ACRYLIC   Acrylic resin. One of the names for several thermoplastic resins known as acrylics or methacryliates. They may be clear, crystalline, opaque, or colored.

ALPHA CELLULOSE   Chemical treatment is used to create this pure form of cellulose. It can be used as a filler in urea and melamine resins.

BLOW MOLDING   A technique that forces hot air into a hollow plastic tube while it expands and conforms to the shape of the mold's cavity.

CALENDERING   The forming or producing of plastic sheet and film by compressing it to uniform thickness between counterrotating rollers.

CAST/CASTING   The forming of plastics without pressure by pouring the fluid resin into molds that are then baked and cured. After it has hardened into the desired shape, it is removed and machined.

CAST PHENOLIC RESIN   A thermosetting resin formed by pouring a fluid solution of phynolformaldehyde into open molds, allowing it to harden while baking at temperatures of 60° to 100° Celsius. It was popular for jewelry in the 1930s and 1940s.

COMPRESSION MOLDING   A method of producing thermoplastics by using a two-part mold. The molding compound is placed into the lower half of a preheated steel cavity. The upper half of the mold is lowered and set into place. Heat and pressure are then applied over several minutes, which forces the compound to take the shape of the inner surface of the mold. In the final step, the plunger is lifted and the molding is ejected.

EDGE LIGHTING   Diffused light enters one edge of a transparent sheet, often made of plastic. The surface must be clean, polished, and parallel in order to reflect the opposite edges. Polystyrene and acrylics are popular materials for this use.

FABRICATING   The technique of finishing off plastics by using machining rather than casting or molding.

FLOW MARK/FLOW LINE   An imperfection on the surface of a molded object due to improper flow of the resin into the mold. Usually identified as a wavy surface.

FORMALDEHYDE   A basic ingredient used in some thermosetting resins. It is a clear, colorless gas usually used as a solution in water.

FRP   Fiberglass-reinforced plastic. The layering of reinforcing fiber and plastic in an open mold. Reinforcing resin is often done by hand and then allowed to cure for a few minutes before the next layer of plastic is applied.

INJECTION MOLDING   A molding process whereby a heat-softened plastic material is rammed into a fairly cool, closed cavity to cure and then is quickly ejected.

LAMINATE   A plastic material made up of layers of resin-impregnated paper, fiberglass, asbestos, cloth, or linen that have been bonded together using heat and pressure to form a single sheet. Laminates are used in many ways, including the facing for tabletops and cabinets. They are applied with special adhesives and applied to wood and other surfaces.

MOLD/MOLDING   Molding material is placed inside an open cavity. The inner surface of the cavity will form the outside shape of the final product. Molding begins when a plunger forces the molding material against the inside of the mold.

MOTTLE   A variegated or speckled coloring in plastics created by processing different colored stocks together or by the addition of fillers such as cloth fibers or wood flours.

NATURAL PLASTICS   Resins and other substances derived from animal or plant sources that have molding properties. Examples include amber, a fossilized tree resin; shellac, an insect secretion; and animal protein substances such as tortoiseshell, horn, and ivory.

NYLON   A thermoplastic resin that can be injection-molded as well as formed into fibers and yarns.

PLASTIC   A synthetic organic compound known as a polymer that can be shaped with heat and pressure.

POLYSTYRENE   A thermoplastic polymer obtained from ethylene. It offers clarity and a wide color range and is primarily used for housewares, toys, and packaging.

POLYVINYL CHLORIDE (PVC)   A thermoplastic resin derived from a gas that results from the reaction of acetylene and hydrogen chloride. PVC is widely used in furniture made from its electrical insulation pipe forms.

THERMOFORMING   The heating of a thermoplastic sheet that is then forced down onto a mold surface by either compression or vacuum action, or both. When cool it holds the mold's shape.

VINYL   Synthetic thermoplastic resins, including polyvinyl chloride (PVC).

Plastic Trademarks

MELAMINE (melamine-formaldehyde)

Catlin Melamine	Catalin Corp.
Formica	Formica Insulation Co.
Melantine	Ciba Products Corp.
Melmac	American Cyanamid Co.
Melurac	American Cyanamid Co.
Micarta	Westinghouse Electric and Manufacturing Co.
Plaskon Melamine	Allied Chemical Corp.
Resimene	Monsanto Chemical Co.
Watertown Ware	Watertown Manufacturing Co.

POLYETHELENE (polythene)

Alathon	E. I. Du Pont de Nemours
Carlona	Shell Chemicals
Fortiflex	Celanese Corp.
Marlex	Phillips Petroleum
Poly-Ethylene	E. I. Du Pont de Nemours
Polythene	E. I. Du Pont de Nemours

POLYSTYRENE

Amphenol	American Phenolic Corp.
Bendalite	Bend-A-Lite Plastics
BP Polystyrene	BP Chemicals
Beetleware	American Cyanamid (Beetle Products Co. England)
Cibanold	Ciba Products Corp.
Daka-ware	Harvey Davies Molding Co.
Durez Urea	Durez Plastics and Chemical Co.
Formica	Formica Insulation Co.
Lamicoid	Mica Insulator Co.

Plaskon	Allied Chemical Corp.
Plastaloid	Smith-Gaines, Inc.
Rauxite	US Industrial Alcohol Co.
Rhonite	Rohm and Haas Co.
Uformite	Resinous Products and Chemical Corp.
Urac	American Cyanamid Co.

VULCANITE (ebonite, hard rubber)

Cohardite	Connecticut Hard Rubber Co.
Endurance	American Hard Rubber Co.
Mercury	American Hard Rubber Co.
Navy	American Hard Rubber Co.
Resiston	American Hard Rubber Co.

VINYL, PVC

Elasti-glas	S. Buchsbaum Co.
Elvax	E. I. Du Pont de Nemours
Famenol	General Electric Co.

Sources

SHOWS

Baby Boombazaar, P.O. Box 8822, Madeira Beach, FL 33738—(813) 398-2427

Sanford L. Smith and Associates, 68 East Seventh Street, N.Y. 10003—(212) 777-5218

Atlantique City (world's largest indoor antiques and collectibles show)
Atlantic City, NJ, Convention Center, usually last week in March
Brimfield Associates, P.O. Box 1800, Ocean City, NJ 08226—(609) 926-8484

Molly's Manhattan Show and Sale of Vintage Fashion and Antique Textiles, 200 Fifth Avenue at the 200 Club, New York, NY; October 23 and April 30
Contact: Molly Turner—(413) 549-6446

Triple Pier Expo, November 13 and 14; November 20 and 21; Pier 88
Contact: Stella Show Management—(201) 386-0010

Vintage Clothing, Estate and Costume Jewelry Show and Sale, October 2 and 3
Contact: The Young Management Co.—(203) 758-3880

Vintage Fashion Expo, September 25 and 26, Oakland Convention Center, Oakland, CA
Contact: (510) 653-1087

Pacific Northwest Vintage Fashion Market, November 5, 6, and 7, Seattle Flag Pavillion, Seattle, WA
Contact: Somewhere in Time Promotions—(206) 848-5420

APPRAISERS

Noble House, Carol and Jerry Dinalli (toy specialists), 124 East Cook Street, Libertyville, IL 60048—(708) 367-8588

AUCTION HOUSES

Butterfield and Butterfield, 220 San Bruno Avenue, San Francisco, CA 94103

Christie's New York, 502 Park Avenue, New York, NY 10022

Christie's East, 219 East 67th Street, New York, NY 10021

William Doyle Galleries, 175 East 87th Street, New York, NY 10128—(212) 427-2730

Du Mouchelles, 409 East Jefferson, Detroit, MI 48226—(313) 963-0248

Leslie Hindman Auctioneers, 215 West Ohio Street, Chicago, IL 60610—(312) 670-0010

Illustration House (twice yearly; original illustration art, movie, magazine, etc.), 96 Spring Street, 7th Floor, New York, NY 10012-3923—(212) 966-9444

Skinner, Inc., Bolton Gallery, 357 Main Street, Bolton, MA 01740

Sotheby's, 1334 York Avenue, New York, NY 10021

Treadway Gallery, 2029 Madison Road, Cincinnati, Ohio 45208—(513) 321-6742

John Toomey Gallery, 818 North Boulevard, Oak Park, IL 60301—(708) 383-5234

BACK ISSUE BOOKS, MAGAZINES

Book Castle, Inc. (books, posters, back-issue magazines), 200 North San Fernando Boulevard, Burbank, CA 91502—(818) 845-1563

DEALERS

Boomerang, David Pinson, mid-century and Postmodern design. In association with John Toomey Gallery, 818 North Boulevard, Oak Park, IL 60301—(708) 383-5234

Decades A Go Go, Dan Rubin, 1514 East 7th Avenue, Ybor City, FL 33605—(813) 248-2849

Metropolis, Wade Herman, (813) 823-2939

Have a Nice Day, 6907½ Beverly Boulevard, Los Angeles, CA 90036—(213) 937-6067

Private Estate Liquidators, Inc., Jimmy Lamena, 445 East Palmetto Park Road, Boca Raton, FL 33432—(407) 338-9999

Decor Moderne, Yvon Belisle, 2101 N.E. 14th Avenue, Wilton Manors, FL 33305

Elan and Elan, Jeff Greenberg, 345 Lafayette, New York, NY—(212) 529-2724

Fifty/50, Mark Isaacson, 793 Broadway, New York, NY 10003—(212) 777-3208

Lost City Arts, James Elkind, 275 Lafayette Street, New York, NY 10012—(212) 941-8025

Moderne Antique, 1812 Maryland Avenue, Baltimore, MD 21201—(410) 685-8999

Catalina Productions, Sheila Steinberg, 200 East 65th Street, New York, NY, 10021—(212) 832-8228

Modern Times, Martha Torno and Tom Clark, 1536 North Milwaukee Avenue, Chicago, IL 60622—(312) 772-8871

Partners in Time, 66 Jobs Lane, Southhampton, NY 11968—(516) 287-1143

Uniquities, Francine Cohen, (201) 763-1778

A Alpha Antiques, Susan Dods, Somerset, NJ—(908) 220-8880

Skank World, Linda Gershon, 7205 Beverly Boulevard, Los Angeles, CA 90036—(213) 939-7858

The Time Machine, William LeMaster, 906 N.E. 19th Avenue, Fort Lauderdale, FL 33304—(305) 462-1551

ITALIAN GLASS

Ripley's Antique Galleries, 1502 West McCarty Street, Indianapolis, IN 46221—(317) 264-5034

METALS

Cecil Skillin, 111 Caribbean, Naples, FL 33963-2795

Imagination Unlimited (silver only), specializing in Georg Jensen, 4302 Alton Road, #820, (305) 534-5870, Miami Beach, FL 33140

Matchmaker of Iowa, P.O. Box 43, Waterloo, IA 50704

Mrs. Kay's, P.O. Box 291245M, Los Angeles, CA 90029

Replacements, Ltd., 1089 Knox Road, P.O. Box 26029, Greensboro, NC 27420

Tere Hagan, Box 25487, Tempe, AZ 85285

MUSEUM COLLECTIONS

Art Institute of Chicago, Michigan Avenue at Adams Street, Chicago, IL

Black Fashion Museum, 126th Street, New York, NY

Brooklyn Museum, 200 Eastern Parkway, Brooklyn, NY

Cooper-Hewitt Museum, 2 East 91st Street, New York, NY

Cranbrook Academy of Art Museum, 500 Lone Pine Road, Bloomfield Hills, MI

The Detroit Institute of Arts, 5200 Woodward Avenue, Detroit, MI

Emerson Museum of Art, 401 Harrison Street, Community Plaza, Syracuse, NY

The Haeger Potteries, Seven Maiden Lane, Dundee, IL 60118-2397

Houston Contemporary Arts Museum, 5216 Montrose Boulevard, Houston, TX

77006 Association, Houston, TX

Los Angeles County Museum of Art, 5905 Wilshire Boulevard, Los Angeles, CA 90036

Metropolitan Museum of Art, Fifth Avenue at 82nd, New York, NY 10028

Museum of Modern Art, 11 West 53rd Street, New York, NY 10019

Museum of the City of New York, Fifth Avenue at 103rd Street, New York, NY

The Newark Museum, 40 Washington Street, Newark, NJ

Wadsworth Atheneum, Hartford, CT

MUSEUMS OUTSIDE THE UNITED STATES

Les Musee Des Arts Decoratifs de Montreal, Canada
Design Museum, London, England
Victoria and Albert Museum, London, England

NEWSLETTERS

The Vintage Gazette (quarterly newsletter of vintage clothing),
194 Amity Street, Amherst, MA 01002

ORIGINAL POSTER ART

Illustration House (original illustration art, movie posters, etc.),
96 Spring Street, 7th Floor, New York, NY 10012-
3923—(212) 966-9444

POSTERS

Separate Cinema (black movie posters), John Kisch, Box 114,
Hyde Park, NY 12538—(914) 452-1998
Miscellaneous Man (mail-order), George Theofiles, New Free-
dom, PA—(717) 235-4766, fax (717) 235-2853
Poster Graphics Inc., Peter Langlykke and Robert Perrin, 376
South County Road, Palm Beach, FL 33480—(407) 833-8448

RENTALS

Modern Props, Michael Ladish, 4063 Redwood Avenue, Los Angeles, CA 90066—(310) 306-1400

TEXTILES, DESIGN STUDIO DISPLAYS

Jack Denst Designs, 7355 South Exchange, Chicago, IL 60649—(312) 721-5155, fax (312) 721-5515 (old patterns can be seen and ordered through decorators)

Jack Lenor Larsen Design Studio, 232 East 59th Street, New York, NY 10022

Ben Rose Designs, Space 11-123, Merchandise Mart, 222 Merchandise Mart Plaza, Chicago, IL 60654—(312) 467-6253

VINTAGE CLOTHING

Jezebel, 1980 East Sunrise Boulevard, Fort Lauderdale, FL—(305) 761-7881

Antique Lace and Textiles, 31 Gage Street, North Westminster, VT 05101—(802) 463-4958

Harriet Love, 412 West Broadway, New York, NY 10012—(212) 966-2280

Bibliography

CERAMICS

Perry, Barbara et al. *American Ceramics: The Collection of the Everson Museum of Art*. New York: Rizzoli International, 1989.

Clark, Garth. *American Ceramics: 1876 to the Present*. New York: Abbeville Press, 1987.

Donhauser, Paul S. *History of American Ceramics: The Studio Potter*. Dubuque, Iowa: Kendall/Hunt Publishing Co., 1978.

FASHIONS

Lobenthal, Joel. *Radical Rags: Fashions of the Sixties*. New York: Abbeville Press, 1990.

Martin, Richard and Koda, Harold. *Flair: Fashion Collected by Tina Chow*. New York: Rizzoli International Publications, 1992.

FURNITURE

Gandy, Charles D. *Contemporary Classics: Furniture of the Masters*. New York: Whitney Library of Design, 1990.

Habegger, Jerryll and Osman, Joseph H. *Sourcebook of Modern Furniture*. New York: Van Nostrand Reinhold, 1989.

Stimson, Miriam. *Modern Furniture Classics*. New York: Whitney Library of Design, 1987.

GLASS

Adlerova, Alena. *Contemporary Bohemian Glass*. Prague: Odseon, 1979.

Buechner, T.S. and Warmus, W. "Czechoslovakian Diary." *Journal of Glass Studies 23*. Corning, New York: The Corning Museum of Glass, 1981.

Charleston, Robert J. *Masterpieces of Glass (A World History from Corning Museum of Glass)*. New York: Harry N. Abrams, Inc., 1990.

Frantz, Susanne K. *Contemporary Glass*. New York: Harry N. Abrams Publishers, 1989.

Grover, Ray and Lee. *Contemporary Art Glass*. New York: Crown Publishers Inc., 1975.

Klein, Dan. *Glass: A Contemporary Art*. New York: Rizzoli, 1989.

Klein, Dan and Lloyd, Ward. *The History of Glass*. London: Orbis, 1984.

Littleton, Harvey. *Glass Blowing: A Search for Form*. New York: Van Nostrand Reinhold Co., 1971.

Madigna, Mary Jean. *Steuben Glass: An American Tradition in Crystal*. New York: Harry N. Abrams, Inc., 1982.

Newman, Harold. *An Illustrated Dictionary of Glass*. London: Thames and Hudson, 1977.

Perrot, Paul N., Gardner, Paul V. and Plaut, James S. *Steuben: Seventy Years of American Glassmaking*. New York: Praeger Publishers, 1974.

Stenett-Willson, Ronald. *Modern Glass*. New York: Van Nostrand Reinhold Co., 1975.

Berkeley Pop Culture Project. *The Whole Pop Catalog*. New York: Avon Books, 1991.

Bony, D. Anne. *Les Annees 60*. Paris: Editions du Regard, 1983.

Castleman, Riva. *The Prints of Andy Warhol*. New York: Abbeville Press, 1993.

DeLorenzo, Alan and Counord, Christine. *Jean Prouve/Serge Mouille*. Paris: J. R. Impressions, 1986.

DiNoto, Andrea. *Art Plastic*. New York: Abbeville Press, 1984.

Harling, Robert, Ed. *Modern Furniture and Decoration*. New York: Conde Nast Publications Ltd., 1971.

Lippard, Lucy R. *Pop Art*. New York: Praeger World of Art Paperbacks, 1966.

McFadden, David Revere. *Scandinavian Modern Design 1880–1980*. New York: Harry N. Abrams, Inc., 1982.

McNulty, Lyndi Stewart. *Price Guide to Plastic Collectibles*. Dubuque, Iowa: Wallace-Homestead, 1987.

Miller, R. Craig. *Modern Design in the Metropolitan Museum of Art (1890–1990)*. New York: Harry N. Abrams, Inc., 1990.

Le Musee Des Arts Decoratifs De Montreal. *What Modern Was: Design 1935–1965*. New York: Le Musee Des Arts Decoratifs De Montreal in association with Harry N. Abrams, Inc.

Naylor, Colin, Ed. *Contemporary Designers, 2d ed.* Chicago: St. James Press, 1990.

de Noblet, Jocelyn, Ed. *Industrial Design: Reflections of a Century*. Paris: Flammarion/APCI, 1993.

Schofield, Maria, Ed. *Decorative Art and Modern Interiors: 1974–1975*. New York: Viking Press, 1974.

Tuchman, Maurice. *A Report of the Art and Technology Program of the Los Angeles County Museum of Art (1967–1971)*. Los Angeles: The Los Angeles County Museum.

White, Susanne. *Psychedelic Collectibles of the 1960 and 1970*. Dubuque, Iowa: Wallace-Homestead, 1990.

MEMORABILIA

Handy, Roger, Erbe, Maureen, and Antonier, Aileen. *Made in Japan: Transistor Radios of the 1950s and 1960s*. San Francisco: Chronicle Books, 1993.

Lesniewski, Karen and John. *Kiss Collectibles Identification and Price Guide*. New York: Avon Books, 1993.

Turpen, Carol. *Baby Boomer Toys and Collectibles*. Atglen, Pennsylvania: Schiffer Publishing, 1993.

MAGAZINE

Henkel, David K. *Magazines Identification and Price Guide*. New York: Avon Books, 1993.

POSTERS

Arwas, Victor. *Belle Epoque Posters and Graphics*. New York: Rizzoli International, 1978.

Freeman, Dr. Larry, compiled by *Victorian Posters*. Watkins Glen, New York: The American Life Foundation, 1969.

Fusco, Tony. *Official Identification and Price Guide to Posters*. New York: Ballantine Books, 1990.

Gallo, Max. *The Poster in History*. New York: American Heritage Publishing Co., 1974.

Hutchinson, Harold F. *The Poster: An Illustrated History from 1860*. New York: Viking Press, 1968.

Keay, Carolyn. *American Posters of the Turn of the Century*. New York: St. Martin's Press, 1975.

Barnicoat, John. *A Concise History of Posters: 1870–1970*. New York: Harry Abrams, Inc., 1972.

WOODCRAFT

Jacobson, Edward. *The Art of Turned-Wood Bowls*. New York: E.P. Dutton, Inc, 1985.

Manhart, Marcia and Manhart, Tom, Eds. *The Eloquent Object*. Seattle: University of Washington Press, 1987.

Nakashima, George. *The Soul of a Tree: A Woodworker's Reflections*. New York: Kodansha International, 1981.

Smith, Paul J. and Lucie-Smith, Edward. *Craft Today: Poetry of the Physical*. New York: Weidenfeld and Nicolson, 1986.

MUSEUM CATALOGS

Dale Chihuly Japan 1990. Tokyo: Japan Institute of Arts & Crafts, 1990.

Index